I0487259

Solving for Technology

How to quickly learn valuable new skills
in a madly changing technology world

David Clinton
Bootstrap IT

Solving for Technology

How to quickly learn valuable new skills in a madly changing technology world

David Clinton

ISBN: 978-1-387-51766-4

Contents

Chapter 1

Managing change

You might as well get used to it. in all likelihood, the pace of technology change will probably not slow within your lifetime. Whether it's new devices, new delivery platforms, or the new coding paradigms and operating system tools to control them, it makes no sense to assume your current skills are going to be enough to stay afloat. At some point, you're going to need some new tools.

To get a handle on the problem, it's probably a good idea to start by asking yourself two questions:

- Within the context of your current work and long-term career goals, how exposed are you to technology-influenced disruption?
- How can you most accurately identify the kinds of new skills you should be looking to add to your portfolio?

I'll try to help you answer those questions in this introductory chapter. The rest of the book will focus on addressing other problems: section one (chapters 2-4) will explore some powerful learning *methodologies* you can use, section two (chapters 5-6) will introduce you to some powerful learning *tools* that you could adopt, and section three (appendices 1-3) is meant to expose you to the basics of some core infrastructure tools like Linux and AWS administration and TCP/IP networking.

Ready to go?

1.1 Why your career needs future proofing

So then, just "how exposed are you to technology-influenced disruption"?
Well that depends on what you do for a living. Here are some general
thoughts:

- If you write programming code professionally, you'll definitely want
  to keep an eye on industry trends. You might be a world-class authority on BASIC or Pascal, but if there just aren't that many companies
  hiring hordes of BASIC and Pascal developers for their new projects,
  expect the demand for work opportunities to remain low. Based on
  your current skills, are you even sure your *present* employer will have
  work for you a year or two from now?

- If you administrate on-premises bare-metal servers for a living, expect trouble. The number of leftovers may never quite hit zero,
  but most locally maintained data center workloads will probably be
  migrated to a public cloud platform like Amazon Web Services in
  the near future. And as virtualization continues to change the way
  servers run, the legacy infrastructure that remains local will probably require fewer human hands to administrate it.

- If you manage information technology (IT) operations or teams of
  developers - or make decisions affecting those operations - you'll need
  a way to intelligently evaluate what's currently available. You'll also
  need to anticipate new stuff that's just coming on-line. It must be
  demoralizing to receive detailed reports from expert stakeholders
  outlining the choices you face but have no way to judge for yourself
  whether it all makes sense. What happens when they ask you for
  your opinion?

- If you're looking to launch your career and trying to figure out the
  best way to sell yourself, you'll need some profile depth. Trust me,
  a CV with just "Javascript developer" in the Skills section doesn't
  sound nearly as good as "Javascript developer with AngularJS and
  Apache Cordova experience on Docker-based microservices apps."

The bottom line is that the things you learned in school or during that
three-month stretch between jobs five years back won't keep you going
indefinitely. You're going to have to crack open the books eventually. You
might as well invest a bit of time up front to make sure that when you do
it, you do it right.

1.2   What you should be learning

Don't expect *me* to tell you what you should be learning. That's *your* business. But I can offer a few thoughts that, assuming you're still undecided, should help you figure it out for yourself.

First of all, make a point of keeping an eye on IT trends. What compute platforms appear to be growing more popular? Where are the IT giants like Amazon and Google investing their big bucks? Which programming languages show growing demand among published online job ads?

An excellent tool for researching trends is Google Trends. Figure 1.1 below shows a search comparing worldwide search patterns for Kubernetes (the open source container administration system) and vSphere (VMware's virtualization platform) over the last five years. As you can clearly see, vSphere isn't going anywhere anytime soon, but interest growth in Kubernetes is definitely sustained. Scrolling down through the page will also show you interest by region.

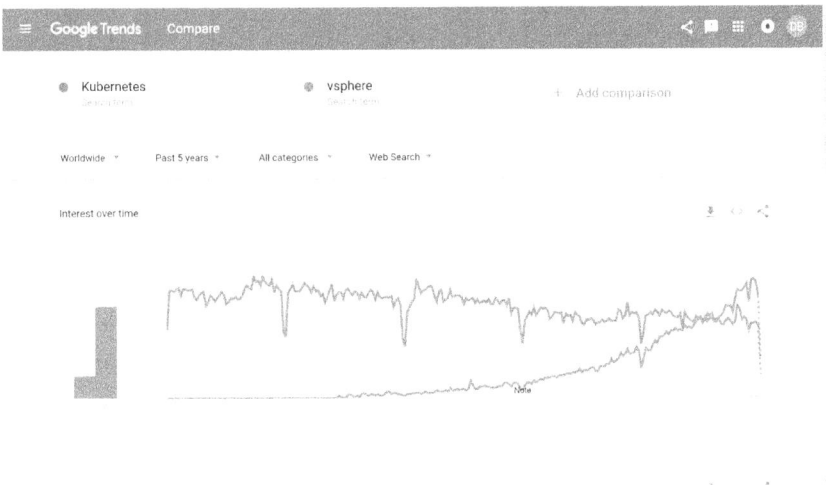

Figure 1.1: A sample Google Trends search comparing interest over time in two popular virtualization platforms

Accurately assessing trends, however, can be tricky. Thousands of people might express some desire to learn about a new programming language, for instance, but that doesn't mean that companies are about to start investing in projects built on it. No projects...no career benefits for you.

And we've all seen technologies whose sudden meteoric rise in popularity is followed just as suddenly by a steep fall.

To do this right, you'll also need to regularly follow at least one technology news feed like Ars Technica, Tech Crunch, or (my favorite) ZDNet. It also won't hurt to stay up to date with events in the worlds of politics, business, and economics - each of which can have a significant impact on the kinds of ventures that organizations might undertake.

Some time back, I was offered a job with a large and well established technology company. The fact that I was familiar with the history behind the technology in question (and with the fact that that particular company had arrived very late to the party) made my decision to turn down the offer easier. It was equally obvious that investing time learning their tools made little sense. Being informed helps.

Whenever possible, try to incorporate big tent technologies into your learning. By "big tent" I mean the larger environments within which applications and IT services are run. And by "larger environments" I mean platforms like Linux (which currently dominates the enterprise and web server markets), Amazon Web Services (AWS - which currently dominates the cloud computing market), and Android (which currently - as of May, 2017 - accounts for more than two billion monthly active mobile devices).

Why are big tent technologies so important? Because those are the places where things happen. If you have a solid understanding of how they work, you'll be far more effective at whatever it is you're trying to accomplish.

Avoid getting trapped inside silos. AWS is a terrific place to build infrastructure for secure and highly reliable services, but two or three years from now? Who knows...once upon a time IBM's lock on the PC and business server market also appeared unassailable.

Similarly, strive to at least understand the underlying design and structure of one or two programming languages besides the one you use for most of your work. Java and Python are both great today...but what would your career prospects look like if you only knew how to code in COBOL?

You don't want your narrow knowledge to trap you on a sinking ship. On the other hand, of course, if you spread yourself too thin and fail to truly *master* at least one area, then you'll have no ship at all. And I should at least note that, years after the official "death" of a technology (like COBOL), some experts will still receive desperate calls from companies needing fixes for copies running it on their legacy systems.

Balance. Everything is balance.

To add some more value to this chapter, I'm going to briefly describe some of those big tent technologies and why you might want to learn a bit more about them.

1.2.1 Cloud computing

Cloud computing is the provision of on-demand (meaning self-service) compute, memory, and storage resources remotely over a network. A lot of the cost-effectiveness of the cloud model is the result of the fact that usage charges are calculated and billed in very small increments (often in fractions of a penny).

This makes it possible to launch risky projects because there's no need to purchase, build, and house all the expensive hardware you'd need to properly support traditional IT stacks. Instead, you effectively "rent" just enough equipment to handle changing demand on your site and pay only for what you actually end up using. As shown in figure 1.2, properly configured, your cloud resources will automatically "scale" up and down according to demand, resulting in minimal wastage and, often, significant cost savings.

Microsoft (Azure), Google (Google Cloud Platform), and even Alibaba (Alibaba Cloud) offer robust cloud services, but Amazon's AWS (Amazon Web Services) remains absolutely dominant, both in terms of market share and the sheer range of services they provide.

Given how quickly enterprise, government, and organizational deployments are being migrated to cloud platforms of one flavor or another, it's only a matter of time before you're asked to participate. You won't want to look stupid, right?

1.2.2 Web development

Crafting good code and reliable, secure infrastructure is something to be proud of. But don't get all snobby about it and forget that, more often than not, you'll also need to expose your service to the customers/clients who will use it. That will usually mean building some kind of web interface through which your product can be attractively displayed and consumed.

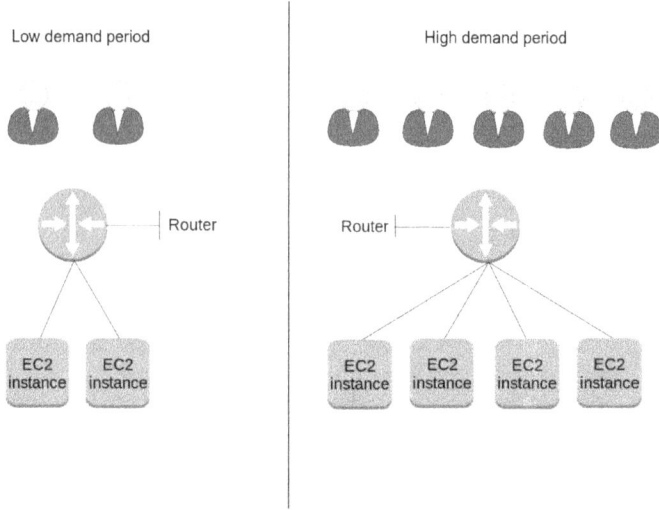

Figure 1.2: Elastic systems can dynamically add or remove resources to meet changing demand

Getting that done will require working through a few layers of web development. Just in case you're not yet familiar with how all that works, here are some of the tools you'll need to know:

- **Hypertext Markup Language (HTML).** The text annotation standard that, being understood by web browsers, allows them to present HTML files to users in an attractive and readable form. Basic HTML is not hard to learn, but is as essential to web communication as English is to the world of flight and air traffic control.
- **Cascading Style Sheets (CSS).** CSS documents can be used alongside HTML to closely define the way HTML elements should be visually laid out and presented to users. While most CSS functionality could, technically, be included within HTML files, keeping them separate allows for a more efficient and modular document design.
- **JavaScript.** Web site interactivity - through which visitors can engage with the site content by customizing the display, entering data, and initiating transactions - is usually provided through programming using the event-driven language, JavaScript.
- **HTML5.** Most discussions of "HTML5" aren't referring to the fifth major version of the HTML standard as such, but to the new ways that this version handles multimedia and cross-platform mobile

clients. Because so much web traffic is now coming through small-screen mobile devices, and because the outdated Flash multimedia standard is so hopelessly buggy and insecure, modern web sites *must* incorporate HTML5 technology...or else.

- **PHP**. You can add significant scripting power to a web page - to permit relatively smooth and simple database integration or access to host resources - through the PHP server-side scripting language. PHP code snippets are often embedded directly within HTML code, so implementation is closely connected to website creation.

- **LAMP**. The overwhelming majority of modern websites are powered by one version or another of LAMP server. LAMP stands for "Linux, Apache, MySQL, and PHP", although you can substitute another web server package (like Nginx) for Apache, a different SQL-based database (like MariaDB) for MySQL, and Python for PHP. Being comfortable quickly building, configuring, and securing a LAMP server can make you a real hero with your development team. My Linux in Action book from Manning includes a number of chapters that cover those topics in depth.

1.2.3   Databases

Most applications generate data, and data - especially when it comes in large volumes - must be properly organized and maintained if it's going to be useful.

A relational database (like MySQL, MariaDB, or Amazon's Aurora) organizes data into *tables* made up of *columns* and *rows*. The Structured Query Language (SQL) is a standardized syntax for managing data on relational databases. A *database engine* (like MariaDB) is software for managing relational database data and exposing it to administrators and automated processes using SQL syntax.

For applications that must quickly process updates but don't require a high level of data consistency (for instance, online gaming applications), you might prefer a NoSQL database engine like MongoDB or Amazon's DynamoDB.

But either way, being comfortable working with data can make you far more effective - and popular - as a developer or admin.

1.2.4   Big data

Think about this:

- There are millions of web-based applications running right now, cheerfully chugging along doing their thing.
- There are billions of Internet of Things devices (like your smart fridge or car) cheerfully doing *their* thing.
- Each application and device can easily output many megabytes of data in a day.

Cumulatively, they're producing unimaginable volumes of data. Who's going to read it all? How can it be put to use? Data analysts, data engineers, and machine learning specialists, that's who. If your background overlaps one of those areas, and a project you're working on interfaces with large data streams, consider adding a related technology like R, MongoDB, or MapReduce to your portfolio.

1.2.5   Docker

Containers are extremely lightweight virtual servers that, rather than running as full operating systems, share the underlying kernel of their host OS. Containers can be defined using plain-text scripts, created and launched in seconds, and easily and reliably shared across networks. Figure 1.3 illustrates the basic container model.

Docker is currently the best known container technology out there and is largely responsible for a revolution in application delivery. Networked services are now delivered through swarms of disposable "immutable and ephemeral" servers whose behavior is tightly scripted and integrated through software front-ends like Kubernetes or Docker's own Docker Swarm Mode.

Because of the particular ways they live and die, containerized applications will often need special handling at the coding stage, so the more familiar you are with Docker structure, the faster you'll be up and running in a container world.

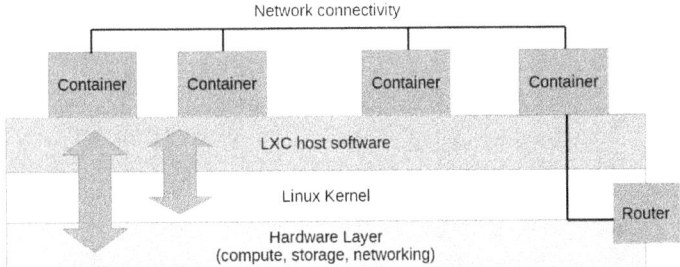

Figure 1.3: Containers live on physical host servers, sharing host resources by way of a specially modified OS kernel

1.2.6 Blockchains

People can't seem to stop talking about cryptocurrencies like Bitcoin these days. But within the IT world, most of the big action is probably going to happen around blockchains - the underlying technology that makes Bitcoin work.

A blockchain, represented below by figure 1.4, is a distributed string (or "chain") of records used to validate transactions. The idea is that maintaining a reliable and incorruptible public "ledger" of transactions can greatly improve the way many businesses function. And those businesses will need plenty of developers and administrators to create and manage the new infrastructure. Why not join in?

1.2.7 Security and Encryption

Everyone's infrastructure is vulnerable to attack. From teenagers and their smart phones to massive corporate data center campuses: if there aren't multiple layers of protection in place, expect service disruptions. To be honest, even if there *are* multiple layers of protection, there will still

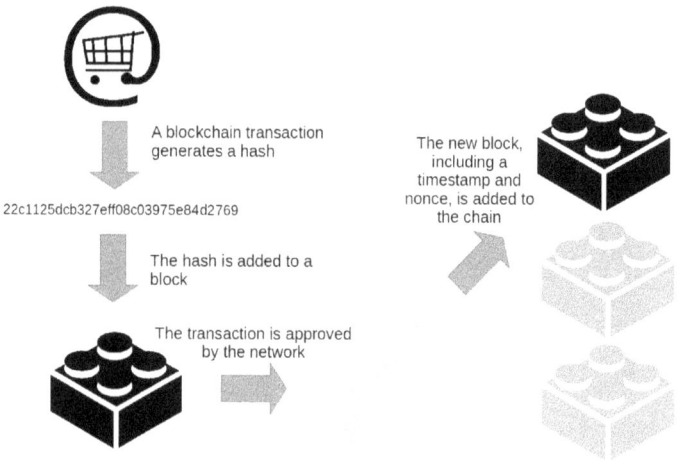

Figure 1.4: The step-by-step representation of a blockchain transaction

be service disruptions, just fewer.

Someone's got to design, test, and implement security protocols and encryption algorithms. And someone's got to build firewalls and convince people to use proper passwords and multi-factor authentication. These are jobs that every organization needs done, and that need isn't disappearing any time soon.

1.2.8   DevOps

DevOps isn't a technology per se - it's actually more of a process - but it's popular enough throughout the programming world these days to justify your attention.

DevOps (formed from the words "Development" and "Operations") promotes collaboration between a project's development, Quality Assurance (QA), and IT teams that's designed to facilitate faster time-to-deployment and software update cycles, and to allow greater levels of process automation.

Often the true benefits of automation come through the use of continuous delivery tools like Ansible or Amazon's AWS CodeDeploy. Being able to simply plug new or updated code into a kind of virtual assembly line with all the underlying infrastructure and compatibility details invisibly taken care of can speed things up, improve quality, and reduce errors. Figure 1.5 shows the cycle of a typical DevOps workflow.

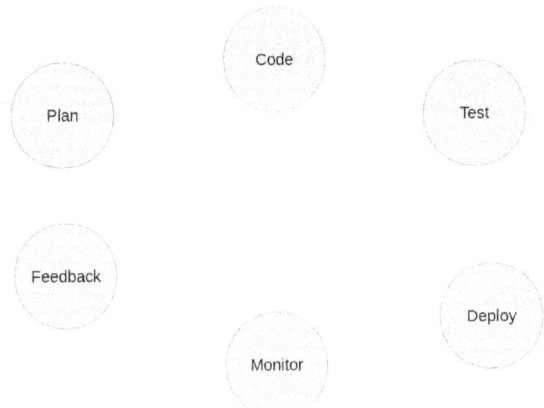

Figure 1.5: The continuously repeating DevOps cycle

If you think you'll ever join an organization that uses DevOps methodologies, you'll want to be familiar with the basic process and philosophy so you can hit the ground running.

Chapter 2

Thinking it through

In this chapter, you're going to learn about...

- Choosing technologies that fit your background and professional needs.
- Finding technologies that come with resources and external support to help with your learning goals.
- Optimizing your learning plan to best maintain enthusiasm and interest.

Everyone dreams, and some dreams eventually translate to plans. Once in a while, it must be said, a plan even inspires some soft stirrings of movement. But achievement? Let's not get carried away.

Growth is hard. Nevertheless, there are things that we can control that can help the process along. You'll always need a certain mental toughness and discipline - things I'm not sure can be taught - so that'll be your responsibility. But there are techniques and tricks specific to technology learning for staying motivated and finding the right frame of mind. Those, as illustrated in figure 2.1, are what we'll talk about in this chapter.

Choosing the Right Technology

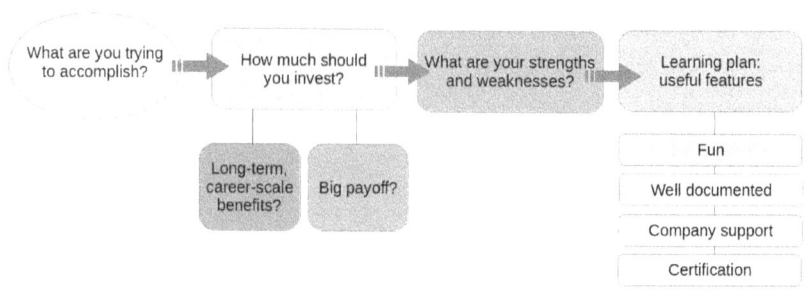

Figure 2.1: A decision flow that might produce smart learning choices

2.1   Identifying the problem that needs solving

Before plunging head first into your next learning adventure it's worthwhile taking a moment to ask yourself a few questions. Being clear about *why* you're doing something can improve the *way* you go about it. The idea is to design a learning plan for yourself that's a comfortable fit both with where you are now and where you want to be in a year or two.

First off, what exactly do you hope to gain from this new technology? What's currently missing in your career or knowledge stack that this skill will fix?

Are you a system administrator who sometimes struggles to understand the needs of the developers you serve, or a developer who sometimes wants to launch your own test environments to see how your application will actually run? Can you hear the clock ticking on your current job and you'd like to leverage your existing skills to quickly pick up new ones?

How can this kind of clarity help? Well, for one thing, it'll certainly make it less likely that you'll end up wasting time by investing in something that won't end up being helpful. But the big "savings" will come from knowing how deep you should dig.

Here's an obvious example. If you're considering a career in Linux administration, then you should look for a curriculum covering a full range of Linux tools (like my Linux in Action book, for instance). But if you're only interested in picking up the tools you need to safely provision and launch your web application, then you might be better off with a simple how-to guide - the kind that a web search for *install web app on lamp server* might uncover.

You should also try to calculate the potential payoff: if learning a particular new technology will likely get you a job with a considerably higher salary, then it might be worth spending the time and money on longer courses and even studying for certification exams. But if, on the other hand, the benefits are less dramatic, then you might want to limit the scope of your studies and pursue them in your spare time.

Perhaps most important of all, you should make sure that your new learning project is a good match for your particular strengths and background. Ambition is great, and pushing yourself out of your comfort zone can be rewarding for a thousand reasons. But if, say, the *day-to-day work* of a sysadmin - or of a Java developer - has never attracted you, then it's foolish to allow an *unrealistic ambition* to push you into something that you'll probably regret.

I don't know about you, but I've known plenty of people whose dreams drove them to catastrophic failures. Take a cousin of mine as an example of doing it right. He really thought he'd love to be a dentist and he had the intelligence and drive to do it. But before making his final decision, he spent a week sitting in a dentist's office and watching. At the end of the week, his mind was set: the work wasn't for him. (In case you're wondering, for the past twenty five years or so, he's been practising successfully as a physician.)

Contrast my cousin with the many professionals - including a nice handful of dentists - I've known who chose badly and, within a few years, usually end up washing out.

Again: when everything is said and done, the plan has to fit the problem - *your problem* - that it's meant to solve.

2.2   Squeezing the most out of your learning

If you'll bear with me just a bit longer, I'd like to explore a few more thoughts on choosing. We'll get to actual study tools and best practices soon enough, but some things simply work better when they've been fully planned in advance...and education is one of them.

Let's imagine that you've narrowed your next-tech options down to a short list of topics that nicely match your background, needs, and understanding of market trends. What kind of filters can you now apply to single out the best choice?

All things being equal, these considerations should show you that all things are not equal.

- Just anticipating that you'll enjoy the learning is important. Naturally, other factors like previous familiarity with a technology's larger environment can make a difference. As an example, a background in Linux LXC containers will make learning Docker easier. But there's nothing like enthusiasm to help push back the darkness. So if the only distinguishing characteristic between two options is your excitement for one of them, choose excitement every time.

- Old is the new new. Sure, everyone loves working with cutting edge stuff. But getting up to speed quickly on your own will require documentation, and a tech that's already been around for a while is probably going to have more wikis, guides, how-to's, and Stack Overflow threads than something just out of the gate. Even a vendor's official documentation tends to be a bit rough during its early stages. Getting in early to help out with bug reporting and documentation is wonderful, but if you're looking to make a fast start, stick with a more mature product. Remember: your time is also a significant cost.

- There's another benefit with learning at least some mature technologies: unexpected employment opportunities. There may not be a broad and sustained market for COBOL programmers, but if there's a company (or, more likely, government department) in your neighborhood who happens to be running legacy infrastructure whose admins recently retired, then someone with COBOL experience might just find a happy landing. that's not to say that you should necessarily invest too much time in a technology as old as COBOL, but it does illustrate another potential benefit of working with older platforms. A little creative planning might sometimes pay off.

- Not enough spare time to learn? Ask your boss: your company might just let you take an online course or do research on their time. Some companies actively encourage such studying, often earmarking a set percentage of your monthly work hours to learning new skills. Even better, many organizations have enterprise accounts with the more established online learning platforms - like Pluralsight.com, where my courses live - providing their employees with unlimited access to courses and other tools.

- A good certification can make it easier to convince employers or clients that you know what you're doing. But it could also help get you to the point where you actually do know what you're doing. That's because, as I often like to say, a well designed certification is it's own reward. More often than not, carefully working through a cert's published exam objectives will automatically connect you with the core topics you'll need through real-world daily use of the tool, and introduce you to the features and functions you're likely to need. Having said that, certs have historically worked best within the IT domain - for system administration, networking, and security tasks - more than for programming languages.

2.3 Staying inspired

You know how it goes. A few days after starting a new learning project, you find yourself stuck in the weeds of complex syntax and confusing layers of folders and configuration files. Your exciting long-term dreams feel a long way off and your enthusiasm is beginning to fade. Well I never told you it would be easy, right? Expect tough times and plan for them.

Here are a couple of ideas you can incorporate into those plans.

2.3.1 Learn it backwards

Consider breaking some rules. Don't work through all the topics and domains of your technology sequentially, moving from simple to complex and memorizing abstract details stripped of their practical context. Instead learn the details, but only as they become useful as part of practical and fun projects.

Really? Is that something you can get away with? Can you seriously avoid rote learning and memorization when trying to grasp a new technology? Aren't there just too many fundamental details you need to know up front before you can get any real work done?

Perhaps. Unless, of course, you find a way to keep track of the details while working on practical, satisfying, and compelling tasks. As long as you end up covering all the bases, no one gets hurt.

This was the philosophy I employed while writing my Learn Amazon Web Services in a Month of Lunches and Linux in Action books with Manning. The idea was to introduce the reader to real-world projects pretty much right from the first chapter, while making sure that, by the time the book's done, we've checked all the boxes. Here's how I described it in Linux in Action:

> *Don't worry, all the core skills and functionality needed through the first years of a career in Linux administration will be covered - and covered well - but only when actually needed for a practical and mission critical project. When you're done, you'll have learned pretty much what you would have from a traditional source, but you will also know how to complete more than a dozen major administration projects. And be comfortable tackling dozens more.*

See if you can't find a way to do that with *your* learning projects.

2.3.2   Learn it in pieces

Break large projects down into smaller, logical steps. That way, even if you haven't yet managed to produce a final working product, you'll nevertheless be able to confidently point to the components you did complete. Having successfully worked through 80% of the task sounds and feels a whole lot better than staring at a pile of half-baked failed attempts. And it gives you a solid foundation from which you can move on to the next 20%.

A variation of this approach is to spend a few minutes/hours before starting a project taking a good bird's-eye-view look at all the things you're going to need to do. Pick out the low-hanging fruit - the things that you already mostly understand or for which you've found easy documentation - and focus on those first. If you properly document your successes the way I'll show you in the next chapter, you can take some satisfying and effective shortcuts.

2.4 Maintaining a balanced, healthy lifestyle

You know: eat and sleep well, exercise, get out from time to time, stay in close touch with family and friends...and call your mother. You promised you would.

2.5 Case study

You've all been good kids so far, perhaps I'll tell you a story to help illustrate what we've been discussing.

Kevin has been a senior developer with a small retail grocery chain for a couple of years. Until now, he's primarily been responsible for the internal inventory tracking system. But his company has now grown so large and complex that it makes sense for them to directly integrate their Linux-based inventory system with the supply chain infrastructure used by their vendors. To get that done, Kevin will need to hire a few more developers and assign them individual tasks.

We don't care about all the dirty details that Kevin will need to address to make everything work. But his desire to learn how DevOps tools might make the job more efficient and effective does interest us. Thinking it through, Kevin has three distinct motivations to explore DevOps:

- Extending his skills beyond just coding to application deployment makes him more valuable to his employer - especially since a successful adoption could save the company quite a lot of money *and* save them from having to hire a new IT administrator.
- Learning how code is deployed to production will allow him to design his code more effectively, as he'll be able to test pre-production versions himself and better understand the impact of design decisions.
- Adding at least one DevOps technology to his portfolio will make him more valuable on the job market.

At his point, Kevin made a wise choice (which I suppose you'd expect, considering that he's a fictional character created by someone as wise as your humble author). He decided to do some informal research up front to see if he could at least figure out what tools and platforms existed and which of them might work best for his needs.

Considering the dozens of options and the many learning resources available, this is no simple task. If he were really smart, I suppose he might have consulted chapter 16 from my Linux in Action.

At any rate, Kevin learned about the continuous integration and continuous deployment methodologies and the ways they can integrate deeply with Git (a tool with which he was already very familiar). He also noted that, whatever he chose, it would very likely turn out to be more than happy playing with the Linux servers the company already used.

Kevin then narrowed his platform options to Amazon's AWS Code Deploy, the Ansible orchestration tool, and simple Bash scripts. Good documentation and plenty of peer support seemed to exist for all three, and they were all "future friendly." How to choose between them?

Although what he read was promising, Kevin quickly eliminated Code Deploy simply because he knew his boss wasn't yet ready to seriously consider migrating company infrastructure to the Amazon cloud. Perhaps one day, though...

That left Ansible and Bash. Ansible had the advantage of being purpose-built for just the kind of projects the company needed done and the was choice most people would probably make. But the learning curve felt a bit steep and, in any case, Kevin isn't most people.

But there was something else that drew Kevin to Bash: Linux administration. Kevin had long been fascinated by the open source operating system's secure, stable, and accessible interface, and he'd always sought to learn whatever he could about it whenever the opportunity arose. Well, here was a prime-time opportunity just staring him in the face...and implementation would cost nothing more than time.

Add to that the chance to learn some deeper Bash scripting skills that could be useful in a thousand ways, and it sounds like a done deal. Kevin cornered his boss in between meetings and told him about his research and the possibilities it had presented. He then asked whether he might be able to use some company time to get up to speed on the relevant skills and if the company happened to already have an account with an online technology training service (like Pluralsight).

One or two green lights later, Kevin dove in. Eager to get a good start and not wanting to bog down in details that weren't immediately necessary, he fired up a virtual Linux environment using VirtualBox where he could freely experiment without worrying about breaking anything important. If something did crash, he'd simply shut down and delete the virtual machine and have another one up and running in a few seconds. Curious about how that works? Be patient. There's more coming in chapter 5.

Kevin used his virtual environments to launch test deployments and work out the configuration parameters one at a time. He would only need to worry about putting it all together and pulling the trigger on a real deployment at the very end of the process, once he'd mastered all the steps.

Chapter 3

Work habits (of the rich and famous)

In this chapter, you're going to learn about...

- Managing bottlenecks in your learning workflow
- Learning from failures, error messages, and logs
- Ensuring future access to your successes by creating smart documentation

3.1 Discipline

I'll bet you figured I'd begin this section with an earnest appeal to your better side. You know: rise before dawn each morning and put in a solid three hours' work before eating a light breakfast - making sure not to drop any toast crumbs into your busy laptop keyboard.

Nope. This one is mostly about taking breaks. Why? Because staring at a single thorny problem for too long can sometimes make it harder to think creatively about it. You're more likely to end up hopelessly running around in cognitive circles. A solution? Take some time off and come back later with fresh eyes.

Of course, that doesn't mean you should spend all the time between now and "later" obsessively checking your social media feeds or catching up with the latest sports scores. I've personally found that that kind of break isn't usually helpful - especially considering that I don't really follow any sports. Rather, doing something productive away from the computer or even focusing for a while on a different element of your project can be remarkably refreshing.

Ok. But where's the discipline part? Well, no matter how well organized and clever you are, it really does all come down to consistency. Sure, redirecting and managing your frustration can help, but no matter how tough things get, if you're not willing to climb back into the saddle and charge back to the battle, and the next battle after that, you won't end up accomplishing much.

This, obviously, is true no matter what you're trying to do in life. But perseverance can be especially valuable while learning to produce and deploy applications. You've probably already noticed that just making something compile or load once doesn't always guarantee it'll work the same way the next time. In this context, *discipline* can mean forcing yourself to test your solutions over and over again using different parameters until you really do understand what's going on under the hood...and why.

So, along with a workflow that's flexible and goal-oriented, never lose sight of the venerable Shampoo Principle: rinse and repeat.

3.2   Experiment...and fail

Nothing beats abject and humiliating failure. No, really. Getting something to work perfectly the first time should be such a disappointment, since it means you haven't really learned anything new about the way your technology is built. And it also means that there's a real disaster waiting for you at some point when your project is already in production. And those hurt much more.

So embrace failure.

Embracing failure, however, doesn't mean building a tolerance - or even a perverse thrill - for pain. Rather, it's about learning how to watch for error messages and unexpected system events, and how to find and interpret log messages.

Example? Seeing a message like "`ImportError: No module named x`" may seem like nothing more than an annoyance at first glance, but it's really just your computer politely telling you that there's a required Python module waiting to be installed. Running `pip install x` will quickly solve that problem.

Your OS will generate vast volumes of log data dutifully reporting on all system events. Just to illustrate how you might access some of that wisdom on a Linux machine, this `journalctl` command will return all recent log entries classified as "error". This can be useful for tracking down errors you know occurred without having to wade through thousands of lines of historical - or trivial - entries.

```
# journalctl -p err --since yesterday
```

Similarly, this next example will return all events relating to the Apache web server service running on Ubuntu. Doing the same thing on a CentOS or Red Hat system would use `httpd` in place of `apache2`.

```
# journalctl -u apache2
```

Avoid copying the code examples you find online in how-to guides and simply pasting them into your project. There are two good reasons for this.

- When you type a command yourself - even if you're just reading it straight off an online source - the structure and logic of the syntax will become more apparent to you. And when you mistype something or leave out a detail, the resulting error message will, I assure you, make you smarter.
- Running code or commands you don't fully understand risks breaking stuff. Like your operating system, or even your credit card account. While most of the code snippets you find online are perfectly fine, it's healthy to assume that the one you're about to copy contains hidden malware, dangerous errors, or elements that simply might not get along well with something else that's running on your system. Always read and understand what everything does *before* running it.

Typing commands yourself also makes it more likely that, on a whim, you'll decide to experiment with small changes. Such curiosity will nearly always lead to good places. Unless, or course, the command you're talking about is the old Unix/Linux `dd` file system administration command. One wrong move with `dd` (often nicknamed "Disk Destroyer") can measurably reduce your long-term changes for happiness.

Having said all that, failed experiments can bring unwelcome consequences.

Besides the risk of crashing your system altogether, playing around with a long line of extensions, plug-ins, and software packages can introduce conflicts and configuration rot. It can also make it hard to figure out exactly what caused a separate failure - or even a success.

In fact, after a while you might find your workstation has become plain old flaky. Without a reliable computer to work with, your productivity will grind to a painful halt.

The solution? Virtualize - the way Kevin did using VirtualBox as a sandbox environment at the end of chapter 2 (and as we'll describe in greater detail once we hit chapter 5). That way, the fallout from errors and bugs is limited to the virtual machine and should have no effect on your physical workstation.

3.3 Take notes

I'm sure you've been here before: something you're working on fails and you spend a few hours madly flailing around as you look for the solution. Finally, after building and rebuilding your environment and trying dozens of configuration setting combinations, it clicks and you're back in business. Exhausted but triumphant, you shut down your laptop and head to bed. It's 3:15 am.

And that's the end of the story. Or at least you thought that was the end of the story. A few months later you run into the exact same problem. Your first reaction is relief: "Well at least this time I know how to fix it." Except that you don't. You search through old code, logs, emails, and even your browser cache for clues, but it's a black hole.

Sound familiar? Well I can (just barely) feel your pain. Sure, it's happened to me, but because I'm now obsessive about fully documenting my operations I can barely remember the last time.

Here's how it should work.

3.3.1 Document

While you're still in "experiment" mode, make frequent copies of your code or commands. That might mean pushing updates to a Git repository, or saving changes to a plain text file. Just make sure that it's a

complete record of your process containing enough information to allow
you to rebuild. You can see an example of notes I created for viewers of my
Pluralsight "Network Vulnerability Scanning with OpenVAS" course here:
bootstrap-it.com/openvas. There are some brief meta directions, but it's
mostly a sequential set of Bash commands.

Now what good will those notes do for you if your system crashes? So
make sure you back up your notes (along with all your other working files)
early and often. Ideally, that should include an off-site backup to a reliable
cloud service like Amazon's S3. Oh, and wouldn't you know it, there are
two chapters - 4 and 5 - covering just such processes in my "Linux in
Action" book.

3.3.2 Test

Tech projects tend to have many moving parts. So before archiving your
notes, you should probably confirm that they genuinely represent the working version.

How? Test them. That is, start over from a fresh environment and apply
the commands or code in the exact sequence and format used in the notes.
If it works as expected, you're in business.

Even better, you've also got yourself some base content from which you
can automate many common tasks. That's coming up next.

3.3.3 Infrastructure automation using scripts

A script, in case you haven't yet been properly introduced, is a text file
containing a list of system-level commands. Here's an example of a simple Bash script that will install and then restart the Apache web server
software on an Ubuntu Linux machine:

```
#!/bin/bash
apt-get update
apt-get install apache2
systemctl restart apache2.service
```

The file, assuming it's called `scriptname.sh` can be made executable and
then run from the command line using these two commands.

```
$ chmod +x scriptname.sh
```

```
$ sudo ./scriptname.sh
```

Of course, scripts can be much longer and more complex than that example, and can be made to do some pretty impressive things. And, of course, scripts can also be written and run on non-Linux operating systems using robust tools like, for instance, PowerShell on Windows. But I think you get the general idea.

I mention the subject here because automation should interest you...and scripts of one flavor or another are at the center of the automation revolution.

Visualize this: you're slaving away day and night learning how Docker containers can be used to deploy your web app. Wisely, you're spinning up VirtualBox servers for your testing. Launching a new Linux VM (based on a cloned image) doesn't take long, but babysitting the operating system through the Docker installation process can kill more than five minutes each time...and those are five minutes you'd rather not lose.

Would you like to cut that down to a single command that will babysit itself and still complete in less than a minute? Script it. For this example, head over to Docker's documentation pages, select the installation instructions for your operating system, note the commands you'll need to run, and then paste them into a script. All done. Although it wouldn't hurt to test it out in action just to make sure.

This isn't the place to demonstrate how all this works any great detail, but I would like to throw a few examples your way just to give you an idea of what's possible.

3.3.3.1   Provision Docker containers using a Dockerfile script

This file - named `Dockerfile` - will load an Ubuntu version 16.04 image, install the Apache web server software, create a simple web page with some content ("Welcome to my web site") to act as your web site root (index.html), and open port 80 to permit incoming HTTP browser requests from the internet. Not bad for just a few lines.

```
FROM ubuntu:16.04

RUN apt update
RUN apt install -y apache2
RUN echo "Welcome to my web site" > /var/www/html/index.html
```

```
EXPOSE 80
```

3.3.3.2 Build a Docker-based WordPress site on AWS Elastic Beanstalk

This single file, named `Dockerrun.aws.json` will launch two Docker containers using a very wide range of AWS infrastructure. The first container will run the MariaDB database engine as a site backend, and the other will host the WordPress program itself.

The two containers will talk to each other and, between them, provide a familiar WordPress web interface. Once the file has been run, all you'll need to do is to head over to the URL Elastic Beanstalk will show you and set up your site.

The process was properly explained in chapter 19 of my "Learn Amazon Web Services in a Month of Lunches".

```
{
    "AWSEBDockerrunVersion": 2,
    "containerDefinitions": [
        {
            "name": "mariadb",
            "image": "mariadb:latest",
            "essential": true,
            "memory": 128,
            "portMappings": [
                {
                    "hostPort": 3306,
                    "containerPort": 3306
                }
            ],
            "environment": [
                {
                    "name": "MYSQL_ROOT_PASSWORD",
                    "value": "password"
                },
                {
                    "name": "MYSQL_DATABASE",
                    "value": "wordpress"
                }
            ]
```

```
        },
        {
            "name": "wordpress",
            "image": "wordpress",
            "essential": true,
            "memory": 128,
            "portMappings": [
                {
                    "hostPort": 80,
                    "containerPort": 80
                }
            ],
            "links": [
                "mariadb"
            ],
            "environment": [
                {
                    "name": "MYSQL_ROOT_PASSWORD",
                    "value": "password"
                }
            ]
        }
    ]
}
```

3.3.3.3   Remotely manage a simple web server using an Ansible playbook

Ansible is a deployment orchestration tool that lets you automate the creation of full software stacks across vast fleets of remote servers. In other words, in theory at least, a single Ansible "playbook" can pretty much handle the administration of thousands of servers distributed across the internet.

The idea is that you compose one or more text files whose contents declare the precise state you want for all the system and application software on a specified machine. When run, the orchestrator will read those files, log on to the appropriate host or hosts, and execute all the commands needed to achieve the desired state.

Rather than having to go through the tedious and error-prone process manually on each of the hosts you're launching, you simply tell the orchestrator to do it all for you.

In this example (shamelessly stolen from chapter 16 of my Linux in Action), Ansible will log into each remote server in your `webservers` group - no matter how many of them there are - and add Apache and a locally sourced index.html file. Finally, it will confirm that the Apache service is running properly.

```
---
- hosts: webservers

  tasks:
  - name: install the latest version of apache
    apt:
      name: apache2
      state: latest
      update_cache: yes
  - name: copy an index.html file to the web root
    copy: src=index.html dest=/var/www/html/index2.html
    notify:
    - restart apache
  - name: ensure apache is running
    service: name=apache2 state=started

  handlers:
  - name: restart apache
    service: name=apache2 state=restarted
```

...And all in a dozen or so lines. Impressed? I sure am.

3.4   Case study

Since we last met him, Kevin has pushed ahead with his Bash-based DevOps explorations. He figures that each of his developers can push their code updates from their laptops to the company Git repository. He can then pull the new code into the virtual machine sandboxes he's using as staging servers. There, his Bash scripts will automatically incorporate the code into a live application which can run test connections with one of your company's vendors.

But something went wrong. The remote connection attempts are all timing out and the helpful IT team at the vendor's location reports that they are receiving data requests from your app, but the replies are failing.

Kevin carefully collects as much information as he can from the vendor and then searches through the logs on his local VM. Looks like a networking problem. Further research confirms that incoming requests to the VM were being blocked by the local NAT network. After some time and frustrating trials, Kevin managed to set up port forwarding through the local router so that traffic originating from the vendor - and only the vendor - would be allowed through.

Now, having read this chapter (at least up to the case study section, I guess), Kevin was careful to immediately document every setting and step he'd used in the process of successfully opening up the network. He also tested his solution from a clean VM, and then backed up the documentation to an off-site location.

Then he spent 20 minutes watching cute cat videos on YouTube. But he'd earned it.

Chapter 4

First steps

In this chapter, you're going to learn about...

- Finding information that can help you confirm whether and how you should be using a technology.
- How software package managers can be helpful for installing tools and when they're best avoided.
- How to poke around under the hood to better understand how a technology is built and how, when necessary, it can be fixed.
- How to devise an appropriate plan of attack as you finally prepare to begin your learning.

Settled on the subject of your next technology adventure? No reason to blindly and recklessly rush in. You'll first want to get a feel for the larger technology ecosystem to see how you can use the information to optimize the way you go about your work. It'll also be useful to organize the technology's layers of complexity and design metaphors in your mind and figure out if it'll even do what you want.

Then you can blindly and recklessly rush in.

So how do you scope out a technology's larger ecosystem? Keep reading.

4.1   The big picture

When starting from scratch I'll almost always run a web search using nothing but the technology's name. More often than not, the first two links I'm shown will be the tech's official website and its Wikipedia page.

Both will probably contain helpful information, but my first stop will usually be Wikipedia. That's because I'm confident that, because of Wikipedia's predictable page format, I'll quickly get to the technology's core function and the product category within which it lives.

To illustrate, here's what the first sentence of Wikipedia's article on PHP told me:

> *PHP is a server-side scripting language designed for web development but also used as a general-purpose programming language.*

On the other hand, here's what the world's biggest encyclopedia had to say about Python:

> *Python is an interpreted high-level programming language for general-purpose programming.*

Both introductions quickly communicate their products' core functions: "server-side scripting..." or "interpreted high-level..." respectively. The in-line links point readers to separate standalone pages devoted to explaining topics like "server-side scripting" and "interpreted language." Reading through those pages will expose you to other tools built to meet similar needs, and to greater insights into the value and purpose of such tools.

What makes that information so important? Because you want to be sure that you're making the right choice and that your learning plan is a good fit for the technology.

This kind of high-level context can be really helpful keeping you focused as you become more familiar with the subject. But spending a few more minutes browsing through the rest of the Wikipedia page and the official documentation site can often add important structural knowledge.

For instance, is the technology integrated with your operating system by default? Is the current stable release going to do everything you need or should you install a beta version? Are there any environment dependencies that might conflict with your current system setup? Is the technology extensible to allow for future growth or customization?

Once you're plugged into the technology, it's time to think about how to plug the technology into your system.

4.2 Software installation

Installing programming language environments or administration tools can get tricky. Even if you've got a good software repository available, there are still loads of choices you'll face. So, if you don't mind, I'll take a couple of minutes of your life to talk about some common options, approaches, and considerations. One day you may thank me.

First of all, if you've never had the pleasure of using a Linux repository, I should describe how they work.

4.2.1 Software package managers

Most Linux distributions ship with software package managers, like APT for the Debian/Ubuntu family and RPM/YUM for Fedora/CentOS. The managers oversee the installation and administration of software from curated online repositories using a regularly updated index that mirrors the state of the remote repo.

Practically, this means Linux users can request a package using a single, short command like `sudo apt install apache2` and the manager will query the online repo, assess necessary dependencies and their current state, download all needed packages, and install and configure whatever files need installing and configuring.

But the real beauty of a package manager is how it actively maintains the overall system stability. For instance, when a patched version of the software is added to an upstream repository, the installed version on your computer will be automatically updated. Similarly, when you decide to uninstall a package you're no longer using, the package manager will invisibly survey the system state and remove only those dependencies that are not being used by any other package.

The concept of curated software repositories and integrated package managers has been so successful that it's been imitated for other operating systems. MacOS users will be familiar with HomeBrew and, more recently, OneGet was launched to manage software on Windows 10. You're

a bit late to the party, but we Linux folk are nevertheless glad you're
finally here.

Considering the reliability and security benefits of using managed software,
you'd normally avoid getting your software any other way. But that won't
always be true.

For one thing, not all software can be found on official repositories (especially non-Linux repos). There will also be times when the release version
that's available in the repos is a bit out of date - something that I've
recently encountered with PHP. Sometimes your project simply requires
customization that isn't possible with official versions.

4.2.2   Alternate sources

I don't think I need to tell Windows users how to download and click on
packages to install them. Explaining how to install Git on your machine
and locate and pull package repos is probably also obvious for anyone
reading this book. On the other hand, describing how to manually compile
from source code using `make` could get a bit *too* detailed for this discussion.

So what's this little section really all about? It's about making sure you're
aware of all the possibilities, including language-specific package managers
like `npm` (for Node JavaScript), `pip` (for Python), and RubyGems (for
Ruby, obviously).

Now you know.

4.3   Environment orientation

If you've had any experience writing code then you'll know how compli-
cated it can be to set up your programming and compile environment.
Even something as simple as getting a text editor or Integrated Development Environment (IDE) just the way you want it can be a challenge.

Since choosing a set of tools can be a personal and project-specific process,
my general advice wouldn't be very helpful. But before digging too deeply
into a project, it's worth doing some reconnaissance. whether you're inclined to select Eclipse, Visual Studio Code, Atom, or Vim, make sure you
understand how it will work within the rest of your stack and where your
code will live.

Understanding where your important stuff gets to: now that's something worthy of some serious discussion. But let me first take a step back and talk about GUI desktop programs.

Full disclosure: I'm a Linux admin by trade and, as a result, I've never met a mouse that didn't make me nervous. The command line shell is where I do most of my work and I would never give up its power and efficiency. In fact, all three (Pbook, Ebook, and HTML) editions of this book were written in a plain text editor and typeset entirely from the command line using Pandoc and LaTeX.

But despite my obviously irrational obsessions, I will ask you to trust me when I say that GUIs have their weaknesses. Software built on graphic interfaces tends to shield critical program files from your view. That can sometimes be convenient - especially for less experienced users.

But when the business of the software you're using is development or administration, then the lack of visibility can be a problem. Sometimes you just need to work directly at the file system level.

With that in mind, it can be useful to devote a few minutes to looking around while you're unpacking a new tool. Using the product documentation and your OS search tools, see if you can find where the tool's configuration, data, and binary executable files are parked.

To get you started, here's what you might find in Linux. By convention, Linux applications usually keep their configuration files within the /etc/ directory hierarchy, program data files within /var/, and binary executables in /usr/. That's the general plan. Expect surprises.

4.4 The "Hello World" test run

Once you've made your choice and installed everything that needs installing, there's only one more step before you can dive into your first serious project: confirm everything's working by running some kind of "Hello World" task.

Many technologies - like AWS's EC2 service illustrated in figure 4.1 come with built-in sample projects and you should be able to find quick starter tutorials online for those that don't. But it's worth asking whether those sample projects can perhaps have more - or perhaps less - to teach us than we might initially think.

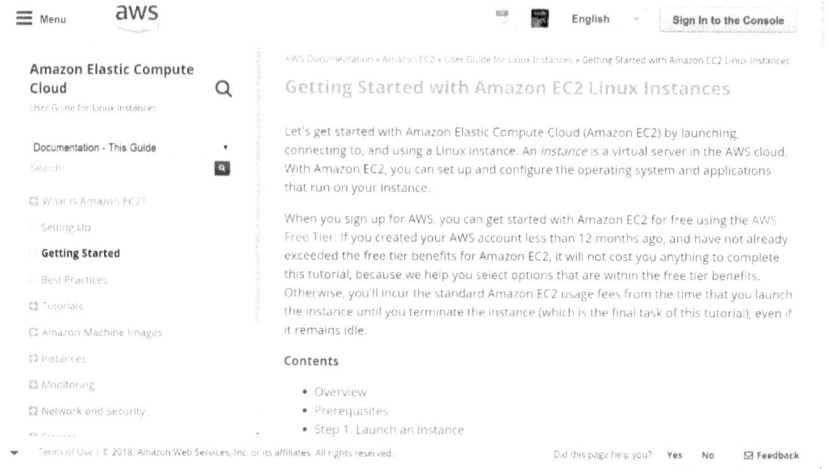

Figure 4.1: An AWS documentation page containing advice for getting started with their EC2 virtual server service

Huh? Well it's kind of a good news, bad news thing.

Let me explain. First the bad news. I've come across a small number of elaborate and official "Hello World" demos that successfully make amazing things happen with just a couple of clicks. But, because everything is so completely abstracted away, they actually teach nothing useful about the technology.

Sometimes the only way to really understand something is to walk yourself through the process the slow and manual way. So if a demo leaves you just as confused as you were before you started, don't take it personally: it might just have been a poorly designed demo. If you want to move ahead with your plans, you may have to take matters into your own hands.

Now for the good news. In many cases, a home-made variation of the "Quick Start" demo can get you most of the way to your goal. Sometimes quickly scanning a getting-started guide for just the key details you're missing can be enough to let you fire up a virtual environment, pull the trigger, and see what happens. Didn't work? Big deal: note the results and try again.

The point is that you don't always need to be carefully walked step-by-step through the process. Sometimes being a bit aggressive can save you loads of time and energy. And the fact that you're working with a disposable virtual machine means that mistakes carry little or no risk.

Of course "scan-and-run" may not be a great idea for full-stack, multi-tier environments like AWS. There, starting at the beginning and working sequentially through a planned curriculum can help you avoid missing critical details — like the way Amazon's billing or security work. Trust me: if you don't like the idea of surprise four-digit monthly service charges or compromised infrastructure, then you don't want to skip the billing and security basics.

So take a moment and think about the scope of the technology you're trying to learn. You could gain important insights into *how* to best approach the problem.

4.5 Case study

As he gets closer to moving his DevOps infrastructure to live production, Kevin realizes he's going to have to focus some attention on security. Since his servers are running Ubuntu Linux, a bit of research tells him that there will be three main firewall alternatives: Ubuntu's own Uncomplicated Firewall (UFW), Iptables, and Shorewall. All, by happy coincidence, are discussed in depth in chapters 9 and 10 of my Linux in Action. Honestly, I'm not sure why Kevin hasn't already gone out and purchased his own copy.

But he hasn't. Instead, he carefully crafted some smart internet search strings that led him to quick-start tutorials for each tool. One at a time, he visually scanned through the guides, copying the key commands he thought would work for his needs. He then launched VMs with his company's applications running, installed and configured a firewall technology and, from a separate computer, tested accessibility, confirming that the right requests were allowed through and the wrong requests were refused.

In the end Kevin decided that Shorewall involved a bit too much of a learning curve, and Iptables seemed a bit too intimidating. UFW hit the mark perfectly. Kevin realized that if his needs had been a bit more complex, then he would have had no choice but to commit to diving deeper in to a more complex or frightening platform. But right now, he's got everything under control.

Chapter 5

Creating a virtual workspace

In this chapter, you're going to learn about...

- Using VirtualBox to provide easily replicated and shared virtual operating system environments.
- Using Linux Containers (LXCs) to provide fast and efficient virtual Linux environments on Linux hosts.

Through the book so far I've dropped enough references to deploying virtual compute environments that even the most stubborn of you must be finding it tough to ignore. "They'll make learning and testing new tools easier, safer, and faster," you've heard me nag.

I'm pretty sure I can even hear some of you starting to weaken: "Why not give it a one-off try if it'll get Clinton to shut up? Just tell me where I can get myself one of those virtual environment thingies."

Fine. You only had to ask.

I'm going to introduce you to Oracle's free VirtualBox cross-platform hypervisor product and, in particular, to the some more advanced tricks for squeezing more value out of your (no-cost) investment. VirtualBox is something you can use on any operating system to create virtualized computers running just about any flavor of Windows or Linux.

You do still have to get a license for any Windows image you decide to run, although you're free to install and use copies without activating the license for a month or so.

If you're using a Linux desktop or laptop, then you might consider installing and using LXC containers instead of - or in addition to - VirtualBox. As long as you're looking for a straightforward Linux server environment, LXC will deliver a surprisingly fast and lightweight experience.

If you've already read my Linux in Action book and some of this material feels a bit familiar, it's because this chapter is a scaled down version of Linux in Action's chapter 2. The content has been made available through kind permission from Manning Publications.

5.1   Getting started with VirtualBox

VirtualBox provides an environment within which you can launch as many virtual computers as your physical system resources can handle. And, of course, it's a particularly useful tool for safely testing and learning new administration skills - which is our primary goal right now.

5.1.1   Installing VirtualBox

Want to try all this out from a Windows PC? Head over to the VirtualBox website and download the executable archive. Click the file you've downloaded and then work through a few setup steps (the default values should all work). Finally, you'll be asked whether you're OK with a possible reset of your network interfaces and then whether you want to install VirtualBox. Of course you are and do.

Getting VirtualBox happily installed on an Ubuntu machine is even simpler. Just two commands:

```
sudo apt update
sudo apt install virtualbox
```

5.1.2   Defining a virtual machine

I'm not sure whether you've ever put together a physical computer from components, but it can get involved. Defining a new virtual machine within VirtualBox works pretty much the same way. The only significant difference is that, rather than having to get down on your hands and knees with a flashlight clenched between your teeth to manually add RAM and a storage drive to your box, VirtualBox lets you define your VM's "hardware" specs by clicking your mouse.

After clicking New in the VirtualBox interface, you will give the VM you're about to build a descriptive name and, as you can see in figure 5.1, the software should be able to correctly populate the Type and Version fields automatically. The Type and Version you select here won't install an actual operating system, but are simply used to apply appropriate hardware emulation settings.

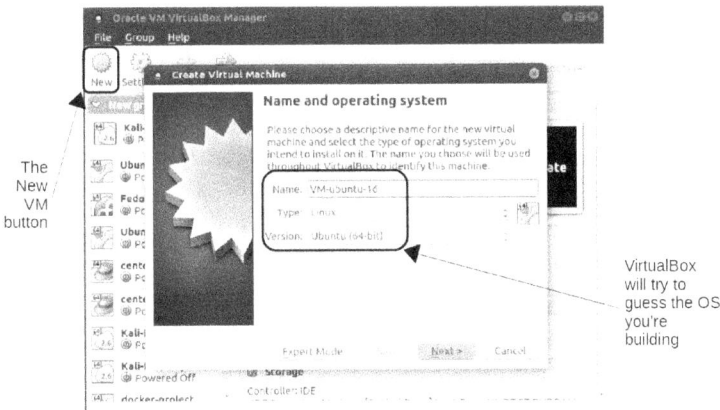

Figure 5.1: The Create Virtual Machine dialog: VirtualBox will try to guess your OS and OS version to offer intelligent default choices later

On the next screen you'll allocate RAM to your VM. Unless you're planning something particularly demanding - like hosting a container swarm or running a busy web server - the default amount (768 MB) should be fine. You can certainly give it more RAM if necessary, but don't forget to leave enough over for your host machine and any other VMs that might already live on it. So if your host only has 4 GB of physical RAM, you probably won't want to give half of that to your VM.

Keep these limits in mind if you eventually decide to run multiple VMs at a time - something that will be useful for testing more complex infrastructure projects. Even if each VM is only using the default amount of memory, two or three of them can start to eat away at RAM needed for normal host operations.

5.1.2.1 Defining your virtual hard disk

What's a computer without a hard disk? The VirtualBox setup process will now ask you if you'd like to create a new virtual disk for your VM or use one that already exists. There may be times when you want to share a single disk between two VMs but for this exercise I'm guessing that you'll want to start from scratch. So select "Create a virtual hard disk now".

The next screen lets you choose a hard disk file format for the disk you're about to create. Unless you're planning to eventually export the disk to use within some other virtualization environment, the default VirtualBox Disk Image (VDI) format will work fine.

I've also never regretted going with the default "Dynamically allocated" option to determine how the virtual drive will consume space on the host. By "dynamic" they mean that space on the host storage disk will be allocated to the VM only as-needed. Should the VM disk usage remain low, less host space will be allocated.

A fixed sized disk, on the other hand, will be given its full maximum amount of space right away, regardless of how much it's actually using. The only advantage of "Fixed size" is application performance, but since I generally only use VirtualBox VMs for testing and experiments, I'm fine avoiding the trade off.

When VirtualBox knows it's Linux you're after - and because Linux makes such efficient use of storage space - VirtualBox will probably offer you only 8 GB of total disk size on the next screen (figure 5.2). Unless you've got unusually big plans for the VM (like, say, you're going to be working with some serious database operations), that will probably be fine. On the other hand, if you had chosen Windows as your operating system, the default choice would have been 25 GB, and for good reason: Windows isn't shy about demanding lots of resources. That's a great illustration of one way Linux is so well suited to virtual environments.

You can also edit the name and location VirtualBox will use for your disk on this screen.

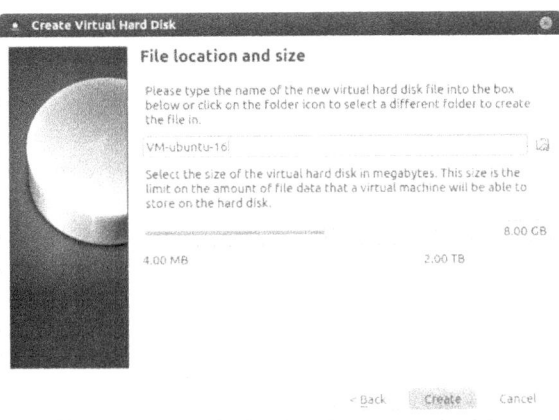

Figure 5.2: If necessary, your virtual disk can be as large as 2 TB - or the maximum free space on the host device

When you're done, click Create and the new VM will appear in the list of VMs on the left side of the VirtualBox manager. Enjoy the taste of success, but you're not done: that was just the machine. Now you'll need an operating system to bring it to life.

5.1.3 Downloading an operating system

Now that you've defined your new VM's virtual hardware profile, here's what still needs doing:

- Download a file (in ISO format) containing the image of the operating system you want to use.
- Boot the new VM using a virtual DVD drive containing the ISO you downloaded
- Work through the standard OS installation process
- Boot the VM and launch the OS you just installed

You'll need to download a .ISO file containing the operating system files and installation program. Finding the right file is usually just a matter of searching the internet for the distribution name and the word "download". In the case of Ubuntu, you could alternatively just go to the https://

ubuntu.com page and click on the Downloads tab as you see in figure 5.3. Notice the various flavors of Ubuntu that are available. If you're going to be using this VM for administration tasks, then the small and fast Server version is probably a better choice than Desktop.

Figure 5.3: The Downloads drop-down on the home page of Ubuntu.com. Note the range of versions Ubuntu offers

5.1.3.1   Validate the ISO archive you downloaded

Large files can sometimes become corrupted during the download process. If even a single byte within your .ISO has been changed, there's a chance the installation simply won't work. Because you don't want to invest time and energy only to discover that there was a problem with the download, it's always a good idea to immediately calculate the checksum (or hash) for the .ISO you've downloaded to confirm that everything is as it was.

To do that, you'll need to get the appropriate SHA or MD5 checksum (which is a long string looking something like this: 4375b73e3a1aa305a36320ffd7484682922262b3) from the place you got your .ISO. In the case of Ubuntu, that would mean going to the web page at releases.ubuntu.com, clicking the directory matching the version you downloaded, and then clicking one of the links to a checksum (like, for instance, SHA1SUMS).

You should compare the appropriate string from that page with the results of a command run from the same directory as your downloaded .ISO that might look like this:

```
$ shasum ubuntu-16.04.2-server-amd64.iso
```

If they match, you're in business. If they don't - and you've double checked to make sure you're looking at the right version - then you might have to download the .ISO a second time.

5.1.4 Installing an operating system

Once your .ISO file is in place, head back to VirtualBox. With the VM you just created highlighted in the left panel, click the green Start button at the top of the app. You'll be prompted to select a .ISO file from your file system to use as a virtual DVD drive. Naturally, you'll choose the one you just downloaded. The new VM will read this DVD and launch an OS installation.

> Most of the time the installation process will go fine. However, describing solutions to each of the many small things that *could* go wrong would require a couple of full chapters. So if you do have trouble you can consult the documentation and guides that are available for your operating system or share your question with the online community.

When everything is nicely installed, there might still be a few more things to take care of before you can successfully boot into your VM. With your VM's entry highlighted, click the yellow Settings icon. Here's where you can play with your VM's environment and hardware settings.

Clicking on Network, for example, allows you to define network connectivity. If you want your VM to have full internet access through the host machine's network interface then, as shown in figure 5.4, you can select "Bridged Adapter" from the Attached drop-down, and then the name of your host's adapter.

> Using a bridged adapter might not always be your first choice, and it might sometimes present a security risk. In fact, choosing "NAT Network" is a more common way to provide a VM with internet access. However a bridged network is the easiest way to gain full network connectivity so, for testing at least, it's a useful approach.

Figure 5.4: The network tab of the Settings screen. You can determine what type of network interface - or interfaces - to use for your VM

These next sections are a bit bonus-y, but who doesn't like free stuff? I'm going to tell you about two related tricks: how to organize your VirtualBox VMs to make spinning up new ones as quick as possible, and how to use the command line to share VMs across a network.

5.1.5   Cloning VMs for quick starts

One of the most obvious advantages of working with VMs is the ability to quickly access a fresh, clean OS environment. But if accessing that environment requires going through the full install process, than I don't see a whole lot of "quickly."

Until, that is, you throw cloning into the mix. Why not keep your original VM in its clean post-install state, and simply create an identical clone whenever you want to do some real work?

It's easy. Take another look at the VirtualBox App. Select the (stopped) VM you want to use as a master copy, click the Machine menu link, and then Clone. You'll confirm the name you'd like to give your clone and then, after clicking Next, whether you want to create a Full clone (meaning entirely new file copies will be created for the new VM) or Linked clone (meaning the new VM will share all the *base* files with its master, while maintaining your new work separately).

Selecting the Linked option will go much faster and take up much less room on your hard disk. The only down side is that you'll be unable to move this particular clone to a different computer later. It's your choice.

Now click Clone, and a new VM will show up in the VM panel. Start it the way you normally would and then log in using the same credentials you set on the master.

5.1.6 Managing VMs from the command line

VirtualBox comes with its own command line shell that's invoked using vboxmanage. Why bother with the command line? Because, among other benefits, it will allow you to work on remote servers - which can greatly increase the scope of possible projects. To see how vboxmanage works, use list vms to list all the VMs currently available on your system. Here's how that looks on my machine:

```
$ vboxmanage list vms
"Ubuntu-16.04-template" {c00d3b2b-6c77-4919-85e2-6f6f28c63d56}
"centos-7-template" {e2613f6d-1d0d-489c-8d9f-21a36b2ed6e7}
"Kali-Linux-template" {b7a3aea2-0cfb-4763-9ca9-096f587b2b20}
"website-project" {2387a5ab-a65e-4a1d-8e2c-25ee81bc7203}
"Ubuntu-16-lxd" {62bb89f8-7b45-4df6-a8ea-3d4265dfcc2f}
```

vboxmanage clonevm will pull off the same kind of clone action I described above using the GUI. Here, I'm making a clone of the Kali-Linux-template VM, naming the copy "newkali":

```
$ vboxmanage clonevm Kali-Linux-template --name newkali
```

That will work nicely as long as I only need to use the new VM here on my local computer. But suppose I wanted other members of my team to have an exact copy of that VM - perhaps so they could test something I've been working on. For that, I'll need to convert the VM to some standardized file format. Here's how I might export a local VM to a file using the Open Virtualization Format (.OVA):

```
$ vboxmanage export website-project -o website.ova
0%...10%...20%...30%...40%...50%...60%...70%...80%...90%...100%
Successfully exported 1 machine(s).
```

Next, you'll need to copy the .OVA file to your colleague's computer. Bear in mind that the file won't, by any standard, be considered small and dainty. If you haven't got network bandwidth to spare for a multiple GB transfer, then consider moving it via a USB device.

Once the transfer is complete, all that's left is, from the remote computer, to import the VM into that machine's VirtualBox. The command is simple:

```
$ vboxmanage import docker.ova
```

Confirm that the import operation worked using `list vms` and try launching the VM from the desktop.

```
$ vboxmanage list vms
"docker-project" {30ec7f7d-912b-40a9-8cc1-f9283f4edc61}
```

If you don't need any fancy remote access, you can also share a VM from the GUI. With the machine you want to share highlighted, click on the File menu and then on Export Appliance.

Next: the mysterious and wondrous world of LXC.

5.2   Working with LXC

VirtualBox is great for running operations requiring kernel access, for when you need GUI desktop sessions, or for testing niche market edge-case operating systems. But if you're on a Linux machine and you just need fast access to a clean Linux environment and you're not looking for any special release version, then you'd be hard pressed to beat Linux Containers.

Just how fast are LXC containers? You'll see for yourself soon enough. But, because they skillfully share many system resources with both the host and other containers, they work like full-bore standalone servers while using only minimal storage space and memory.

5.2.1   Getting started with LXC

Install LXC on your Ubuntu workstation? Piece of cake:

```
sudo apt update
sudo apt install lxc
```

That's it. We're ready to get down to business. The basic LXC skill set is actually quite simple. I'm going to show you the three or four commands you'll need to make it all work, and then an insider tip that, once you understand how LXC organizes itself, will just blow you away.

Why not dive right in and create your first container? The value given to -n sets the name I want to use for the container, and -t tells LXC to build the container from the Ubuntu template.

```
$ sudo lxc-create -n mycont -t ubuntu
```

If you decided to create, say, a CentOS container, then you should make a note of the final few lines of the output, as it contains information about the password you should use to log in:

```
$ sudo lxc-create -n centos_lxc -t centos
[...]
The temporary root password is stored in:
        '/var/lib/lxc/centos_lxc/tmp_root_pass'
```

You will log in using the user name "root" and the password contained in that file. If, on the other hand, your container used the Ubuntu template, then you'll use "ubuntu" for both your user name and password. Naturally, if you plan to use this container for anything serious, you'll want to change that password right away.

Use lxc-ls --fancy to check the status of your container:

```
$ sudo lxc-ls --fancy
NAME     STATE    AUTOSTART GROUPS IPV4     IPV6
mycont   STOPPED  0         -      -        -
```

Well, it exists, but apparently it needs starting. As before, the -n specifies by name the container you want to start. -d stands for "detach" - meaning you *don't* want to be automatically dropped into an interactive session as the container starts.

```
$ sudo lxc-start -d -n mycont
```

Listing your containers should now display something like this:

```
$ sudo lxc-ls --fancy
NAME     STATE    AUTOSTART GROUPS IPV4        IPV6
mycont   RUNNING  0         -      10.0.3.142  -
```

This time, the container is running and has been given an IP address. You could use this address to log in using a secure shell session.

```
$ ssh ubuntu@10.0.3.142
```

Alternatively, you can launch a root shell session within a running container using lxc-attach.

```
$ sudo lxc-attach -n mycont
root@mycont:/#
```

When you're done playing with your new container, you can either run exit to log out leaving the container running:

```
root@mycont:/# exit
exit
```

...or shut the container down using shutdown -h now.

But before you do that, let's find out just how blazing fast LXC containers are. The -h flag I added to shutdown just before stands for "halt". If I would use r instead, rather than shutting down for good, the container would reboot. So let's run reboot and then try to log in again right away to see how long it takes for the container to get back up on its feet.

```
root@mycont:/# shutdown -r now
sudo lxc-attach -n mycont
```

How did that go? I'll bet that, by the time you managed to retype the lxc-attach command, mycont was awake and ready for action. But did you know that hitting the up arrow key in Bash will populate the command line with the previous command. Using that would make it even faster to request a login. In my case, there was no noticeable delay. The container shut down and fully rebooted in *less than 2 seconds*!

> *Linux containers are also really easy on system resources. Unlike my experience with VirtualBox VMs - where running three concurrently already starts to seriously impact my 8GB host workstation performance - I can launch all kinds of LXC containers without suffering any slowdown.*

Now what about that insider tip I promised you? Well, back in a terminal on the host machine (as opposed to the container), you'll need to open an administrator shell using sudo su. From here on in - until you type exit - you will be sudo full-time.

```
$ sudo su
[sudo] password for username:
#
```

Now change directory to /var/lib/lxc/ and list the contents. You should
see a directory with the name of your container. If you've got other containers on the system, they'll have their own directories as well.

```
# cd /var/lib/lxc
# ls
mycont
```

Move to your container directory and list its contents. There will be a file
called "config" and a directory called "rootfs". The "fs" stands for "file
system".

```
# cd mycont
# ls
config rootfs
```

It's the rootfs directory that I really want you do see right now:

```
# cd rootfs
# ls
bin   dev   home  lib64  mnt  proc  run   srv  tmp  var
boot  etc   lib   media  opt  root  sbin  sys  usr
```

All those subdirectories that fill rootfs...do they look familiar to you? Of
course! They're all part of the Linux Filesystem Hierarchy Standard. This
is essentially the container's root (/) directory...but within the *host's* file
system. As long as you have admin permissions on the host, you'll be
able to browse through those directories and edit any files you want - even
when the container isn't running.

There are all kinds of things you'll be able to do with this access, but
here's one that can quite possibly save your (professional) life one day.
Suppose you do something dumb on a container and lock yourself out,
there's now nothing stopping you from navigating through the file system,
fixing the configuration file that you messed up, and getting back to work.
Go ahead: tell me that's not cool.

But it gets better. It's true that the Docker ecosystem has gained many
layers of features and sophistication since the technology moved out from
under LXC's shadow some years ago. Under the hood, however, it's still
built on top of a basic structural paradigm that will be instantly recogniz-
able to anyone familiar with LXC.

Which means that, should you be inclined to test drive the fastest-growing
virtualization technology of the decade, you've already got skin in the
game.

5.3   Writing code on a remote server

Now that you've got those virtual environment thingies all figured out, what can you do with 'em? Well, it's obvious that such setups are perfect for playing with system tools and architectures.

Suppose you're not into system stuff, but you would like a safe place to build applications. What do I mean by "safe?" I'm talking about an environment where you can freely install libraries and dependency packages without having to worry about destabilizing your personal work computer.

But there are limits to how far that can take you. There's a lot going on beneath the surface of IDEs like Eclipse or Visual Studio, and people become very attached to their convenience. But expecting to be able to easily run all those layers of complexity over a remote connection - and especially on a headless remote server - is perhaps a bit ambitious.

But still, wouldn't it be nice to work on the IDE on your laptop and have the code saved, compiled, and run remotely...say, on a hosted VM or cloud instance? That way you could build your applications on the servers where they'll actually be run without having to risk the stability of your own workstation.

It can be done. Generally, the trick is to get your IDE to ride on top of a Secure Shell (SSH) session. For details, search the internet for something like `eclipse edit java code on remote server`.

5.4   Case study

Our old friend Kevin is still hard at work figuring out how to deploy a DevOps workflow for his company's vendor integration. In fact, he's getting close to putting together a full stack solution. Now, however, he's got to find a way to deliver a live demonstration of what he's done to his bosses and representatives of the vendors' companies.

The simplest solution was to clone the two or three VMs he's been using on his own workstation, and copy the archive files over to an available PC running an office over from the CEO. With that done, all Kevin has to do is walk over to the office, invite the CEO and his team in, and run the demo (all the while shaking with fear over what could go wrong).

It went well. Kevin then sends another set of copies to the the vendor's IT team with instructions on how to run the demo for themselves.

Against all odds - and just the way you'd expect a fictional case study to go - everything goes flawlessly.

Yeah, right.

Chapter 6

Leveraging learning resources

In this chapter, you're going to learn about...

- The kinds of online technology learning resources that are available and how to choose between them.
- How to more quickly and effectively find the best internet resources available to solve your problems.

How do you learn best: books? Video courses? Hands-on interactive classes? And what are you usually looking for when you go out hunting for knowledge: fast fixes to immediate problems? Deep understanding of an entire technology? Quick and dirty getting-starting guides?

Whatever it is you're after, you'll be more likely to get it if you're aware of what's out there. So keep your mind open to the many categories of teaching tools that exist, and join me for a tour of the current state of online technology education.

6.1 Books

Books are books. They've been around forever so I doubt there's too much I can tell you about them that you don't already know. And that includes the fact that you can now read them on your phones and Kindles.

But here's a thought you may find useful: the higher-end technology publishers are able to invest months of careful planning and the work of teams of editors and reviewers into their products. Those efforts are likely to deliver more concentrated value than you'll find in other, less meticulous media formats.

So if you're looking for a well-designed curriculum guiding you on a complex journey through a larger technology **and** you're the type that learns well using book-based information, then consider purchasing a dead tree.

Just wait until it comes on sale. Trust me on that one: sooner or later they're *all* discounted.

Are some technology publishers better than others? Well some publishers put a lot more time and money into creating books that comprehensively teach a topic. So going with top tier providers does increase your chances of success. But good books - like the one you're reading right now - can sometimes find their way into the world through all kinds of channels.

Which publishers are in the top tier? Because of my happy ongoing relationship with Manning I'd certainly include them. But No Starch, O'Reilly, and Wiley would also seem to belong.

Now that's just my off-the-cuff impression. There's a very healthy range of other technology publishers out there that shouldn't be ignored, including McGraw-Hill, Que, Addison-Wesley, and Apress. Large corporations like Microsoft and Adobe will often also publish their own high-quality books to help developers and users easily adopt their products.

You should also pay attention to specific "sub-brands" within a publisher's catalog. Manning, as one example, publishes books with consistent and dependable style and scope using the "x in Action" and "Learn x in a Month of Lunches" titles. Similar successful book series include Wiley's "x for dummies" and O'Reilly Media's "x: the missing manual."

If you got along particularly well with one book from a series, the odds are good you'll enjoy the others, too.

6.2 Curated courses

Just like books, training videos are more likely to be effective if they've been carefully planned, designed, and reviewed. Unlike books, a site-wide subscription to an online service can instantly plug you into solutions to *whichever* specific problem you're facing, no matter what the topic. But either way, teaching is a complex skill and, no matter how and where the teaching takes place, the better the teacher, the more you'll learn.

So if you're after good online courses, look first for sites that employ only experienced teachers, plan their course collections to ensure that important topics are covered and that there isn't repetition, and closely edit and review content before it's allowed online. In other words, sites that curate their content.

6.2.1 Who's big in curation?

Pluralsight.com. With some 6,000 courses spread over eight domains (shown below in figure 6.1) and addressing skill-sets from entry-level to advanced, Pluralsight covers a lot of ground. Since expanding its enterprise focus in June 2016, it now serves more than 50% of Fortune 500 companies, where it's common to provide full-access accounts to many or even all employees. I'm biased, of course, since I've got more than a dozen of my own courses on Pluralsight. Pluralsight offers a free 10-day trial and paid accounts for $29 monthly or $299 annually. You can also take free skills assessments to discover the gaps that need filling.

Lynda.com. Any online education company owned by LinkedIn (which, in turn, is now owned by Microsoft) is probably going to be professional and reliable. Like Pluralsight, Lynda has a wide range of courses, although their catalog skews more towards design and creative skills and, by reputation, their courses tend to be a bit more basic and, for the software development courses, perhaps less real-world. Lynda offers a 30-day free trial and, once that's done, will cost you either $19.99 or $29.99 - depending on whether you want access to project files and offline viewing.

CodeAcademy.com. Code Academy provides hundreds of intermediate-advanced coding classes for free, but also has paid tiers. The Codeacademy Pro tier, for instance, gives you more practice resources and a detailed course syllabus for $19.99/month, while Codecademy Pro Intensive's 8-10 week courses include more hands-on practical experience and cost $199/course. Their content isn't video-based, but consists of

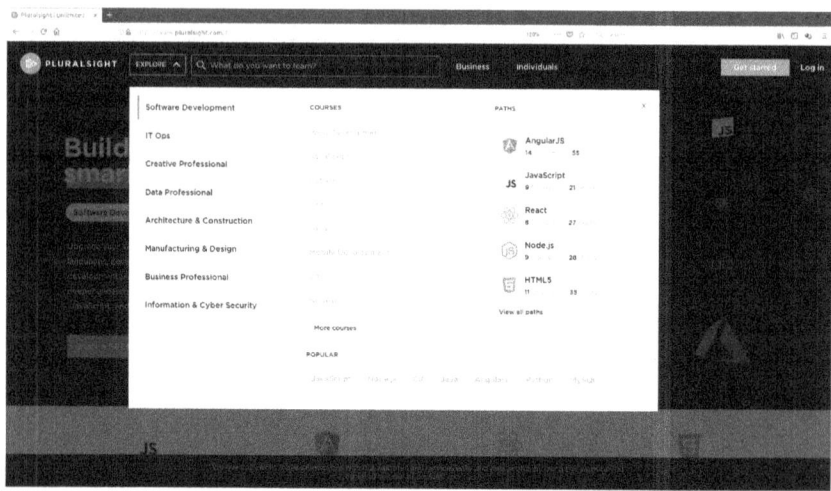

Figure 6.1: Pluralsight's 6,000 courses are divided among eight domains - the largest of which is Software Development

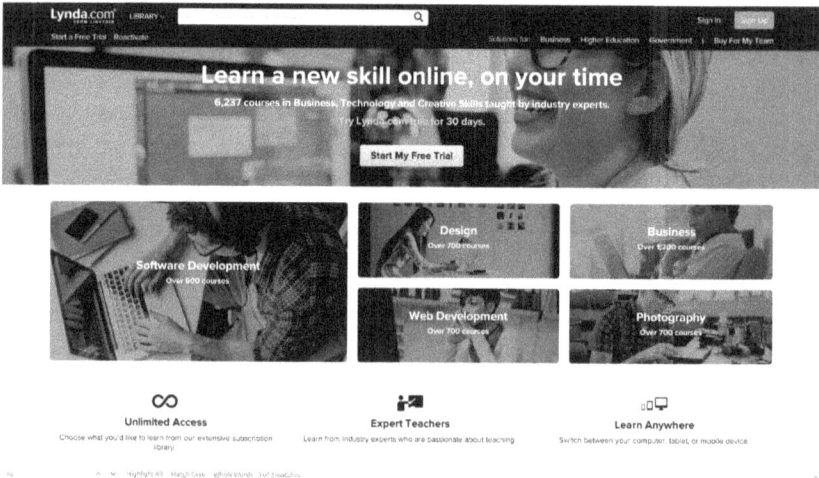

Figure 6.2: The course breakdown by subject at Lynda

text tutorials guiding you through hands-on workspaces. Quite an effective approach, as it turns out.

Treehouse (teamtreehouse.com). By reputation, Treehouse seems primarily aimed at individuals starting out in web design and programming. Besides videos, the site also offers a "Code Challenge Engine" for direct interactive experience. Basic membership costs $25/month and the Pro level goes for $49/month.

freeCodeCamp.org. Like the name says, this one is free. Not just as a way to drive traffic to some kind of revenue-generating web page, but *completely* free because they simply believe such opportunities should exist. The idea is that "campers" work their way through realistic projects centered around coding challenges. But this one is different in a few important ways. For one thing, campers are encourage to join with other local campers so they can code in mutually supportive groups. Once they've worked through the Front End, Data Visualization, Back End, or Full Stack certifications, campers are also encouraged to gain real-world experience by coding for non profits. Finally, freeCodeCamp guides graduates through the job search and interviewing stages of their young careers.

Besides companies offering courses on a full range of tech topics, you'll also find online resources with a more specific focus, like CloudAcademy.com and LinuxAcademy.com. I'll allow you only three guesses as to what each of those is about.

6.3 Non-curated courses

Not sure how to change the bulb on the passenger-side brake light on your 2010 Dodge Caravan (3.8L)? There's a YouTube video that'll show you how. Need to replace the pressure sensor on your ten year old Carrier forced-air natural gas furnace? There's another YouTube video that'll show you how to do that. In fact, there'll be a selection of YouTube videos showing you how to do just about anything you can imagine - and a great many things you couldn't (and perhaps shouldn't).

Got one very specific problem that's blocking your progress? Looking for a bird's eye level overview of your next language? Don't rule out the possibility that someone out there has already been there and recorded the solution in a video. Also, keep an eye out for video authors you liked and subscribe to their YouTube channels. That makes it easier to find more useful content.

Perhaps the most famous and successful YouTube channel of them all is Salman Khan's **Khan Academy**. Although it's primarily aimed at K-12 students, there's plenty there that can be useful for people taking their first steps in programming - or in physics or electrical engineering, for that matter.

The Udemy.com site has many thousands of video courses on all kinds of topics, including technology. Since any author is welcome to upload courses on just about any topic, the collection can't really be considered curated. And video and teaching quality will vary significantly from course to course. But there's enough variety there that spending some time looking around might get you to what you're after. Udemy charges for each course you decide to take.

6.4   Higher education institutions

The costs of traditional higher education programs have ballooned in recent decades. Right now a four year degree in the US can cost you around five times the 2016 median annual *household* income (which was around $59,000). If your degree ends up providing you with $20,000/year income *beyond* what you would have earned without it, it would still take you more than ten years just to break even. And perhaps many more years to pay off the actual debt.

Investments like that don't always make a lot of sense. But suppose you could get the same knowledge at no cost at all?

Welcome to the world of the massive open online course (MOOC). A MOOC is a platform through which an existing educational institution delivers course content to anyone on the internet who would like to consume it.

By joining a MOOC, you can view video recordings of the lectures from the best professors in elite universities and engage in simulated interactive labs at no cost and from the comfort of your own home. In many cases, you can also receive credit or certification confirming your successful completion of a course. Certification often does carry some charges.

The down side - although technically, not everyone will consider this a down side - is that university-based MOOCs will often be less job and industry-focused and spend more time on general theory. They will sometimes also expect you to have already mastered some prerequisite STEM skills.

Here are some major MOOC portals:

Coursera.org. Taking the 4-10 week Coursera courses, along with quizzes and exercises, is free. But they also offer fee-based add-ons including assessments, grades, and certification. *Specializations* are multiple Coursera courses organized into a larger program like Data Science or Deep Learning. To earn a specialization certificate, students must complete a capstone project at the end. Coursera categories include Computer Science, Data Science, and Information Technology.

edX.org. edX is a non-profit organization originally created by MIT and Harvard University whose platform delivers MOOC courseware created by more than a hundred universities and colleges. Students may audit a course for free or, for a reasonable fee, gain verified certificates of completion.

MIT OpenCourseWare. OpenCourseWare isn't really a learning platform and won't help you much if you're looking for an organized guide through a particular topic. Rather, it's an online repository containing notes, quizzes, and some videos from thousands of MIT courses. The content can give you insights into specific questions although, if you're ambitious and determined enough, you could mine entire topics from the rich resources you'll find.

Udacity.com. I included Udacity in this higher education section because that's where its roots lie. But in fact, while the founders came from the Stanford University faculty, the project was originally something of a rebellion against the high costs and distracting bloat of many university degree programs. Rather than spending four+ years studying material that's largely out of sync with the demands of the real job market, why not focus on the skills the industry is looking for and get it done in much less time and for a tiny fraction of the cost?

Today, Udacity offers a couple dozen or so nanodegrees that, with a few months' work, can get to you up to and past entry-level competence in some high-demand fields. Because the nanodegrees are created with the direct involvement of major industry employers like Amazon, Nvidia, and Google, there's a decent chance a hard working graduate will quickly find a great job.

6.5   The open internet

There's a world of help waiting for you out there. Don't miss it.

6.5.1   Learn to compose smart search strings

Internet search is far more than just typing a few related words into the search field and hitting Enter. There's method to the madness. Here are some powerful tips that will work on any major search engine. My own favorite is DuckDuckGo.

6.5.1.1   Use your problem to find a solution

Considering that countless thousands of people have worked with the same technology you're now learning, the odds are very high that at least some of them have run into the same problem you did. And at least a few of those will have posted their questions to an online user forum like Stack Overflow. The quickest way to get at look at the answers they received is to search using the exact language that you encountered.

Did your problem generate an error message? Paste exactly that text into your search engine. Were there any log messages? Find and post those, too.

6.5.1.2   Be precise

The internet has billions of pages, so vague search results are bound to include a whole lot of false positives. That's why you want to be as precise as possible. One powerful trick is to enclose your error message in quotation marks, telling the search engine that you're looking for an exact phrase, rather than a single result containing all or most of the words

somewhere on the page. However, you don't want to be so specific that
you end up narrowing your results down to zero.

Therefore, for an entry from the Apache error log like this:

*[Fri Dec 16 02:15:44 2017] [error] [client 54.211.9.96] Client
sent malformed Host header*

...you should leave out the date and client IP address, because there's no
way anyone else got those exact details. Instead, include only the "Client
sent..." part in quotations:

"Client sent malformed Host header"

If that's still too broad, consider adding the strings Apache and [error]
outside the quotation marks:

"Client sent malformed Host header" apache [error]

6.5.1.3   Be timely

Search engines let you narrow down your search by time. If your problem
is specific to a relatively recent release version, restrict your search to just
the last week or month.

6.5.1.4   Search in all the right places

Sometimes an outside search engine will do a better job searching through
a large web site than the site's own internal tool (I'm looking at you:
Government of Canada). If you feel the solution to your problem is likely
to be somewhere on a particular site – like Stack Overflow's admin cousin,
Server Fault – but you can't find it yourself, you can restrict results to
just that one site:

"gss_accept_sec_context(2) failed:" site:serverfault.com

6.5.1.5   Know what you don't want

Finally, if you see that many or all of the false positives you're getting
seem to include a single word that is very unlikely to occur in the pages
you're looking for, exclude it with a dash. In this example you, of course,
were looking for help learning how to write Bash scripts, but you kept

seeing links with advice for aspiring Hollywood screenwriters. Here's how to solve it:

    writing scripts -movie

6.5.2 Leverage public code samples

Are you stuck in a way that only a developer can be stuck? You've read your code through over and over again and you just can't find the error. You've tried at least a half a dozen different design approaches and even - briefly mind you - an entirely different language. Nothing. The application isn't working.

Haunt GitHub and other places where public repositories of code live. They're all searchable and they're all filled with examples of great code. Of course, there will also be plenty of examples of really bad and even malicious code. Keep your guard up.

Spending smart time browsing through other people's code is a great way to get new ideas and learn about best practices and coding patterns. If your search engine skills are as good as I'm guessing, then you'll probably uncover working solutions to whatever it is that ails you.

6.6 Free stuff

You don't have to do this all by yourself. Before embarking on a significant new learning project, take a good look at your community and government to see what services might be available.

Many governments offer support - both financial and practical - for people looking to upgrade their professional skills. There are also more and more state/provincial governments joining the open textbook movement, where well written and up-to-date technical textbooks are made freely available on the internet. At this point, I would say the quality of most collections looks a bit spotty, but the long-term goal is to cut the cost of an annual education by many hundreds of dollars.

Your company might be willing to sponsor your learning. In fact, many companies provide their employees with accounts to online learning sites and, sometimes, it's just a matter of asking your boss or HR rep about what might be available.

Not that it has to be your company. Check out the **Microsoft Virtual Academy** which, as you can see in figure 6.3, offers all kinds of free courses under three domains: Developers, IT Pros, and Data Pros.

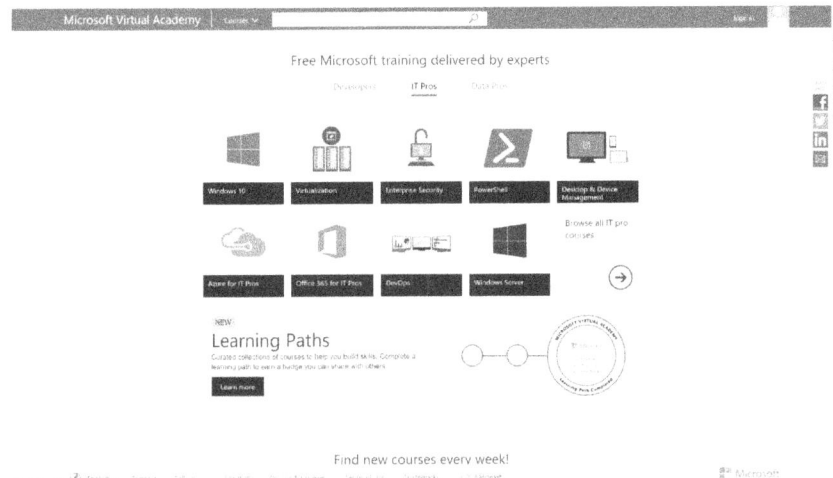

Figure 6.3: Course categories in the IT Pros domain available from Microsoft Virtual Academy

And what about your community? You might be surprised how happy experienced and older professionals are to engage in mentoring. It might take a bit of courage, but go ahead and approach someone you admire to see what wisdom and practical guidance you get.

6.7 Case study

We haven't heard much from Kevin lately. What's he been up to? Believe it or not, he finally finished his research and deployed the new application to integrate with his company's vendors' systems. And with all the time that's been freed up in his schedule, he's started a new learning project: Linux network administration.

But right now Kevin is worried. There have been occasional complaints from users about not being able to connect to the application server. Not many: but a couple last week and four this week. It's a disturbing trend.

It would be nice to get some insight into the server and the software stack running on it.

Kevin got some ideas from internet searches and even some helpful advice from a colleague. But now he's looking for something a bit more comprehensive.

Taking advantage of the new Pluralsight account his company gave him, Kevin browsed the course library to see if there was anything that could help. Well lookie here! There's a brand new "Linux Performance Monitoring and Tuning" course. And the author: David Clinton. Do you suppose we're related?

Chapter 7

Appendix 1: networking basics

I suppose you could say that the core topic of the book has now been addressed and from here on in we're just wrapping up some loose ends. Perhaps "loose ends" isn't quite the right phrase. Let's try "bonus material" instead.

I know. This book was supposed to be *about* learning new technology and not the technology itself. But I thought I'd throw in some basic backgrounders for three of the biggest "big tent" technologies of them all: networking, Linux, and Amazon Web Services. No matter what tools you end up learning and working with, it's hard to imagine going through a full IT or dev career without at some point coming face to face with the members of that club.

So we begin with networking, the glue that holds the everything together. And I mean *everything*. Forget the IT world: if networks failed, our banking, transportation, health, and industrial systems would disappear along with them. If you want to build your corner of the modern world, you'd better understand how it will connect to everything else.

The contents of this chapter, made available through the kind permission of Manning Publications, come from chapter 14 of my Linux in Action and chapter 5 from Learn Amazon Web Services in a Month of Lunches.

7.1   Understanding TCP/IP addressing

A network's most basic unit is the humble Internet Protocol (IP) address, at least one of which must be assigned to every connected device. Each address must be unique throughout the entire network, otherwise message routing would descend into chaos.

For decades, the standard address format followed the IPv4 protocol: each address is made up of four 8-bit octets, for a total of 32-bits (don't worry if you don't understand how to count in binary). Each octet must be a number between 0 and 255. Here's a typical (fake) example:

> 154.39.230.205

The maximum theoretical number of addresses that can be drawn from the IPv4 pool is just over 4 billion (256^4). Once upon a time, that seemed like a lot. But as the internet grew far beyond anyone's expectations, there clearly weren't going to be enough unique addresses in the IPv4 pool for all the countless devices seeking to connect.

> Four billion possible addresses sounds like a big number un-
> til you consider that there are currently more than *1 billion*
> Android smart phones in use—that's in addition to all the mil-
> lions of servers, routers, PCs, and laptops, not to mention Ap-
> ple phones. There's a good chance your car, refrigerator, and
> home-security cameras also have their own network-accessible
> addresses, so something obviously had to give.

Two solutions to the impending collapse of the internet addressing system (and the end of life as we know it) were proposed: IPv6, which is an entirely new addressing protocol, and Network Address Translation (NAT). IPv6 provides a *much* larger pool of addresses but, since it's still not all that widely deployed, I'll focus on NAT.

7.1.1   NAT addressing

The organizing principle behind NAT is both simple and brilliant: rather than assign a unique, network-readable address to every device in your home or business, why not have all of them share the single public address that's used by your router?

But how will traffic flow to and from your local devices? Through the use of *private* addresses. And if you want to divide network resources into multiple subgroups, how can everything be effectively managed? Through network segmentation.

Here's how it works. When a browser on one of the laptops connected to your home WiFi visits a site, it does so using the public IP address that's been assigned to the DSL modem/router provided by your ISP. Any other devices connecting through the same WiFi network use that same address for all their browsing activity (see figure 7.1).

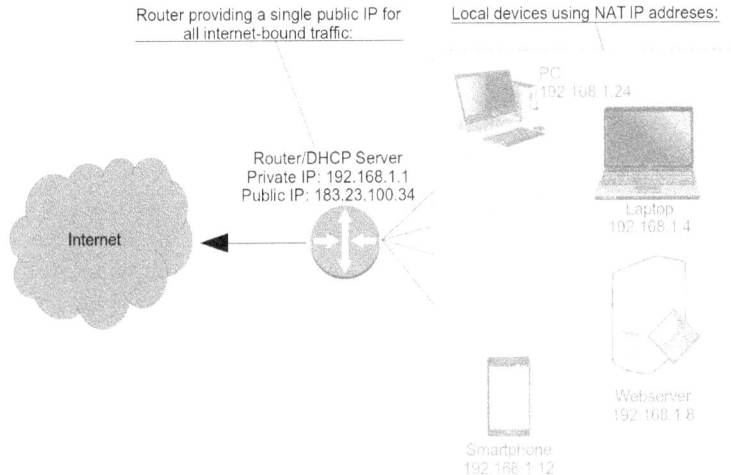

Figure 7.1: A typical NAT configuration, showing how multiple local devices - each with its own private address - can all be represented by a single public IP address

In most cases, the router uses the Dynamic Host Configuration Protocol (DHCP) to assign unique private (NAT) addresses to each local device - but they're unique *only* in the local environment. That way, all local devices can enjoy full, reliable communication with their local peers. This works just as well for large enterprises, many of which use tens of thousands of NAT IP addresses, all behind a single public IP.

The NAT protocol sets aside three IPv4 address ranges that may only be used for private addressing:

- 10.0.0.0–10.255.255.255
- 172.16.0.0–172.31.255.255
- 192.168.0.0–192.168.255.255

Local network managers are free to use any and all of those addresses (there are more than 17 million of them) any way they like. But addresses are usually organized into smaller network (or *subnet*) blocks whose host network is identified by the octets to the left of the address, leaving octets to the right available for assigning to individual devices.

For example, you might choose to create a subnet on 192.168.1, which would mean all the addresses in this subnet would start with 192.168.1 (the network portion of the address) and end with a unique, single-octet device address between 2 and 254. One PC or laptop on that subnet might therefore get the address 192.168.1.4, and another could get 192.168.1.48.

> Following networking conventions, DHCP servers generally don't assign the numbers 0, 1, and 255 to the final octet of a network device's IP address.

Following through with that example, you might subsequently want to add a parallel - but separate - network subnet using 192.168.2. In this case, not only are 192.168.1.4 and 192.168.2.4 two separate addresses, available to be assigned to two distinct devices, but - because they're on separate networks - the two might not even have access to each other (see figure 7.2).

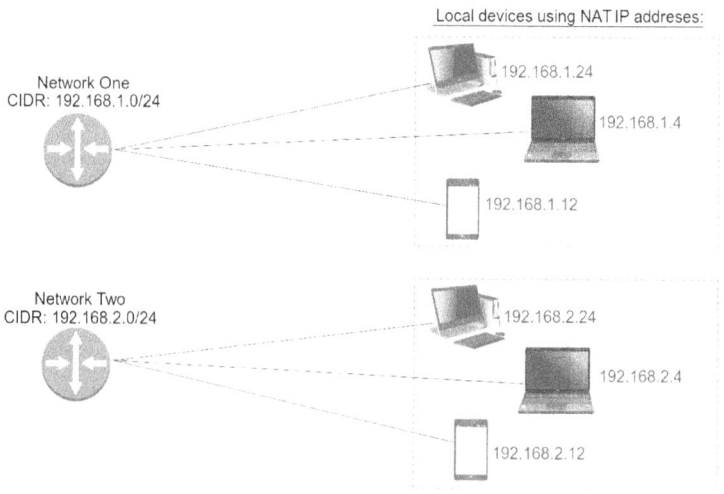

Figure 7.2: Devices attached to two separate NAT subnets in the 192.168.x network range

Because it's critically important to make sure systems know what kind of subnet a network address is on, we need a standard notation that can accurately communicate which octets are part of the network and which are available to be used for devices. There are *two* commonly used standards: *Classless Inter-Domain Routing (CIDR)* notation and *netmask*. Using CIDR, the first network in the previous example would be represented as 192.168.1.0/24: the /24 tells you that the first three octets (8*3=24) make up the network portion, leaving only the fourth octet for device addresses. The second subnet, in CIDR, would be described as 192.168.2.0/24.

These same two networks could also be described through a netmask of 255.255.255.0. That means all 8 bits of each of the first three octets are used by the network, but none of the fourth.

You don't have to break up the address blocks exactly this way. If you knew you weren't likely to ever require many network subnets in your domain, but you anticipated the need to connect more than 255 devices, you could choose to designate only the first *two* octets (192.168) as network addresses, leaving everything between 192.168.0.0 and 192.168.255.255 for devices. In CIDR notation, this would be represented as 192.168.0.0/16 and have a netmask of 255.255.0.0.

Nor do your network portions need to use complete (8-bit) octets. Part of the range available in a particular octet can be dedicated to addresses used for entire networks (such as 192.168.14.x), with the remainder left for devices (or, *hosts*, as they're more commonly called). This way, you could set aside all the addresses of the subnet's first two octets (192 and 168), plus some of those of the third octet (0), as network addresses. This could be represented as 192.168.0.0/20 or with the netmask 255.255.240.0.

Where did I get these notation numbers? Most experienced admins use their binary counting skills to work it out for themselves. But for a short chapter like this, that's a bit out of scope - and unnecessary for the normal work you're likely to encounter. Nevertheless, there are many online subnet calculators that will do the calculation for you.

7.2   Understanding the Domain Name System (DNS)

As your website grows and more people discover it, I'm sure you won't be satisfied with having to identify it by its IP address. A nice, easy-to-remember name like, say, best-site-ever.com will work much better. Let's learn how that works.

Under all those bright, cheerful web pages with external links displayed as softly chiseled 3D boxes and identified by catchy, easy-to-remember names, it's all about numbers. There's no real place called google.com or wikipedia.org; rather, they're 172.217.3.142 and 208.80.154.224. The software that does all the work connecting us to the websites we know and love recognizes only numeric IP addresses.

The tool that translates back and forth between text-mad humans and our more digitally oriented machines is called the *domain mame system*. *Domain* is a word often used to describe a distinct group of networked resources - in particular, resources identified by a unique name like, oh, I don't know, bootstrap-it.com. As shown in figure 7.3, whenever you enter a text address in your browser, the services of a DNS server are invariably - and invisibly - sought.

The first stop is usually a local index of names and their associated IP addresses‘ stored in a file that's automatically created by the OS on your computer. If that local index has no answer for this particular translation question, it forwards the request to a designated public DNS server that maintains a much more complete index and can connect you to the site you're after. Well-known public DNS servers include those provided by Google - which uses the deliciously simple 8.8.8.8 and 8.8.4.4 addresses - and OpenDNS.

Until something breaks, you normally won't spend a lot of time thinking about DNS servers - unless, of course, you want your customers to be able to access your website by its plain-text name. For that to happen, you'll have to reserve the name you'd like with a domain name registrar. The job of a registrar is to update the indexes used by the big DNS servers so that translation requests from anyone on the internet can be quickly satisfied.

Once you're over that critical hurdle, you can go back to ignoring DNS.

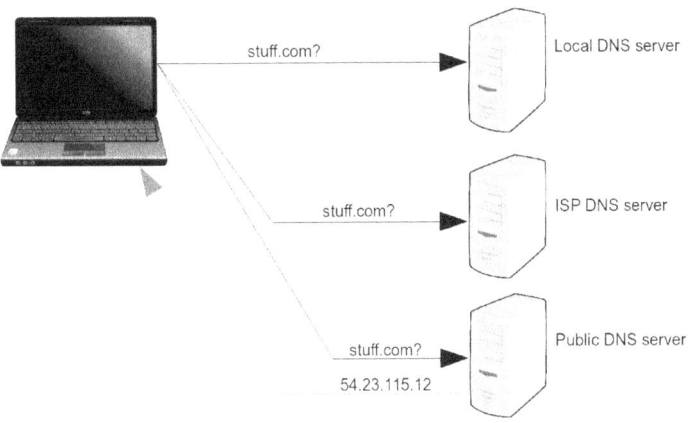

Figure 7.3: DNS address query for stuff.com, and the reply containing a (fictional) IP address

Chapter 8

Appendix 2: basic Linux administration

What's so great about Linux that, back in chapter one, I counted it among my "big tent" technologies? Well let me put it this way: if you're planning to get a workload running on a web server, Internet of Things device, cloud instance, or super computer, then there are overwhelming odds that you'll be working with Linux.

Linux is free, stable, (relatively) secure, infinitely customizable, supported by a solid, mature community and, as you'll soon see, available in permutations built to fit all kinds of use cases. And did I mention it's free? Yes. I believe I did.

So since most technology these days is running on Linux platforms, you're going to need at least a basic familiarity with the way its file system, package management, and security controls are designed.

Of course this is only one short chapter and is no substitute for proper administration skills. What's worse, even according to my own teaching philosophy, this chapter is done all wrong. As I wrote in my Linux in Action book,

> Linux in Action turns technology training sideways. That is, while other books, courses, and online resources organize their content around categories ("Alright boys and girls, everyone take out your slide rules and charcoal pencils. Today we're

going to learn about Linux file systems."), I'm going to use real-world projects to teach.

So, for example, I could have built an entire chapter (or two) on Linux file systems. But instead, you'll learn how to build enterprise file servers, system recovery drives, and scripts to backup archives of critical data - in the process of which, you'll pick up the file system knowledge as a free bonus.

Don't worry, all the core skills and functionality needed through the first years of a career in Linux administration will be covered - and covered well - but only when actually needed for a practical and mission critical project. When you're done, you'll have learned pretty much what you would have from a traditional source, but you will also know how to complete more than a dozen major administration projects. And be comfortable tackling dozens more.

I really think that's the better way to teach this stuff. But I also understand that you're probably not looking for complete immersion right now. So here's the shorter version. 440 pages shorter, to be exact.

8.1   Linux distributions

As I just noted, Linux comes in dozens of flavors called *distributions* (or "distros"). The idea is that you get to choose the distro that's the closest match to your project needs.

Once you start looking, you'll find distros optimized for the cloud, virtual machines, or bare metal servers. There are distros for system recovery, security operations, or cutting edge experimental hardware platforms. There are even consumer distributions for desktops and laptops whose beauty and function will blow you away.

Figure 8.1 should help you choose by showing some of the most popular distributions and their common use-cases.

One caught your eye? Head over to its website, download the appropriate .ISO file, and off you go.

Consider writing your ISO to a flash drive and trying out the OS as a live USB session. You'll get to confirm that the distro runs on your hardware but your fixed data drive will remain untouched.

Linux Distribution Types and Key Examples

Purpose	Distribution
Security/anti-hacking	Kali Linux
Consumer desktop	Mint
Lightweight (great for old hardware and diagnostics)	Puppy Linux
Internet of Things administration	Snappy Ubuntu Core
Enterprise server room	CentOS (community version of Red Hat Enterprise Linux)
Cloud computing	Amazon Linux (AWS AMI) Ubuntu Server
All-purpose (except lightweight)	Ubuntu

Figure 8.1: Common Linux distribution use-cases and popular examples

8.2 Working with root authority

When you first install most Linux distributions, you'll be prompted to create a user account with *theoretical* administration powers. I say "theoretical" because for normal use, you'll only have authority over your own account resources, but not those of other accounts or belonging to the system itself.

But to perform a system administration task that requires editing a system configuration file, you'll need to convince Linux that you've got the authority. To do that, you'll temporarily assume root powers by prefacing you command with `sudo`. Thus, to use the *nano* text editor to open and edit the /etc/group file, you would run this on the command line:

```
$ sudo nano /etc/group
[sudo] password for david:
```

Why not work as root full time? Not a good idea. If your user account were somehow hijacked while enjoying full root privileges, the hijacker would now control the whole system. It's always better to reduce your vulnerable attack suface wherever possible.

8.3 Package managers

One of the greatest pleasures of Linux is the deep and healthy ecosystem of free software that surrounds it. From enterprise-class office suites to professional audio and video editing software to full-featured development tools, there isn't much you can't find among the tens of thousands of available FOSS packages.

But what's even better is the fact that all that software is managed by integrated package managers. What's a package manager? It's a local front end that connects your computer to remote software repositories.

But it's much more than that. The mainstream package managers (in particular APT for Debian/Ubuntu/Mint systems and YUM/DNF for RHEL/CentOS/Fedora) will also...

- Actively *curate* the online repos to remove buggy, outdated, or dangerous packages.
- Install and remove software on request, invisibly ensuring that all dependencies are working.
- Manage the software you've already installed, automatically updating it when necessary.
- Miraculously recover your system state after failed or interrupted managements sessions. I say "miraculously" because there's no other word I can find that accurately describes it.

Here's a 30-second tutorial for Ubuntu's APT. First, update the local index so it'll know what's available upstream. Since this will impact system files, you'll need to use `sudo`.

```
$ sudo apt update
```

If you're not sure of the exact name of the package you're looking for, search for it. This example will return a very long list of candidates with some connection to Git, but as it turns out, the actual Git package is just called git. The [installed] note tells us the current status of the package

```
$ apt search git
git/xenial-updates,xenial-security,
  now 1:2.7.4-0ubuntu1.3 amd64 [installed]
  fast, scalable, distributed revision control system
```

Finally, if necessary, installing Git is as simple as...

```
$ sudo apt install git
```

8.4   SSH: secure remote connectivity

From the looks of you, I'd say you do most of your work on a laptop. But I'd also say that the odds are you're not planning to use your laptop as your web sever. So then how will you configure your server or move your precious applications over? Network connectivity, right?

Sounds great. But are you aware that any data transferred across a public network can be intercepted, read, and modified? The whole thing, passwords and all. Unless, of course, the data is properly encrypted.

The single best way to safely create and encrypt remote connections is using Secure Shell (SSH). The protocol is so good - and so popular - that it's now available not only where you'd expect to see it on Linux and macOS, but even natively on Windows 10.

Here's how it works. We usually refer to your laptop as the *SSH client*, and the server, since it will host your sessions, as the *SSH server*. Make sure that the package `openssh-server` is installed on your server and either `openssh-server` or `openssh-client` on your laptop.

```
$ sudo apt update
$ sudo apt install openssh-server
```

Now, as is illustrated in figure 8.2, opening a new session is as simple as typing `ssh`, the username whose account you'll use on the server (my example is "ubuntu"), and the server's IP address or domain name.

```
ssh ubuntu@10.0.3.141
ubuntu@10.0.3.141's password:
Welcome to Ubuntu 16.04.1 LTS (GNU/Linux 4.4.0-109-generic x86_64)

 * Documentation:  https://help.ubuntu.com
 * Management:     https://landscape.canonical.com
 * Support:        https://ubuntu.com/advantage
Last login: Thu Dec  7 19:01:45 2017 from 10.0.3.1
ubuntu@server:~$
```

That's it.

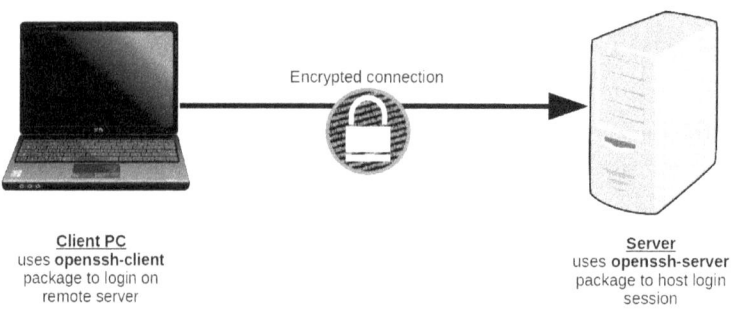

Figure 8.2: Logging in to a remote server through an encrypted SSH connection

8.4.1   Secure file transfer

Now what about that application code sitting on your laptop? OpenSSH has another tool for you: Secure Copy (SCP). Let's say that you've got a Java JAR archive you want to transfer over. Easy. Here's what you'd do from your laptop:

```
$ scp /home/myusername/code/myapp.jar \
  ubuntu@10.0.3.141:/home/ubuntu/
```

You'll be asked for a password for "ubuntu" on the server, and then the JAR file will be dropped into that user's home directory.

How about copying files in the other direction? Suppose you're on your laptop and you want some log files moved from the server to your laptop. Well, assuming the logs are currently in the "ubuntu" user's home directory on the server, here's how that would work:

```
$ scp ubuntu@10.0.3.141:/home/ubuntu/logfiles.zip .
```

The dot at the end tells SCP to save the file to your current directory on your laptop. Try it yourself.

8.5 The Linux file system

Great start. SSH is your way into your Linux server, software is handled via APT or YUM, and you impose your imperial will by invoking sudo. All that's left is learning how to actually do administration stuff Linux.

Remember this single piece of wisdom and you'll never go far wrong:

> *Everything in Linux is a plain text file.*

The trick is simply finding the right files and figuring out what to do with them. So let me introduce you to the Unix/Linux Filesystem Hierarchy Standard.

8.5.1 The Unix Filesystem Hierarchy Standard

With relatively few exceptions, all Linux distros will organize files the same way. To a large degree, you'll find a similar layout on the Unix-based macOS operating system some of you might have heard about. Here's how things look when you list the contents of a typical Linux root directory:

```
$ cd  /
$ ls
bin   initrd.img      mnt    sbin   usr
boot  initrd.img.old  opt    snap   var
dev   lib             proc   srv    vmlinuz
etc   lib64           root   sys    vmlinuz.old
home  media           run    tmp
```

Here's a quick peek inside some of those directories:

- The **/etc/** directory contains configuration files that define the way individual programs and services function.
- **/var/** is where Linux keeps *variable* files belonging to the system or individual applications. These are files whose content changes frequently through the course of normal system activities.
- Individual users are given directories for their private files beneath the **/home/** directory.
- **/lib/** contains shared software libraries.
- The binaries for most command line tools live in **/bin/**.

8.5.2   Getting around

I'm sure you won't have any trouble with this stuff. When you log into Linux - or open a new terminal shell within a GUI session - you'll normally find yourself in your user's home directory. Assuming your user is named ubuntu, this is what running pwd ("present work directory") will look like:

```
$ pwd
/home/ubuntu
```

You can create a new directory within your current location using mkdir and then list the contents with ls:

```
$ mkdir newdir
$ ls
newdir
```

Care to see what's in your new directory? Change to it using cd ("change directory"):

```
$ cd newdir
```

touch will create a new, empty file, and cp will copy it to a new location - or just make a copy of the original with a new name if you don't specify a different location.

```
$ touch newfile
$ cp newfile newerfile
$ ls
newerfile newfile
```

Fed up with all those files taking up space on your hard drive while providing you with nothing in return? Show 'em who's boss and delete one.

```
$ rm newerfile
```

Most of the time, the nano text editor will be installed by default. You can use it to add or change a file's contents. When you're done writing your Great Book, hit CTRL+x to exit, and y to save the file.

```
$ nano newfile
```

Finally, to change to a directory from a different place in the file system, you'll need to include its absolute address, going back to root (/). /var/log/, by the way, is where most system logs are kept. Feel free to take a look around.

```
$ cd /var/log
```

8.5.3 Object permissions

By design, Linux is a multi-user system. That means a single Linux computer can be accessed and used by an infinite number of users and processes concurrently. This is one of the many features that makes Linux so incredibly useful: it allows a level of flexibility and collaboration that has no equal in IT.

But it also means that there's a greater need to protect resources from unauthorized access. You don't want one team of developers to accidentally messing with the config files belonging to another team. And, of course, no one wants the guys in marketing messing with anything.

So all the objects in a Linux file system will have a set of attributes precisely defining who gets to do what. Those attributes - known as *permissions* - are broken down into three categories: read (r), write (w), and execute (x). And users are divided into three classes: the object's owner (u), the object's group (g), and all others (o).

ls -l will display an object's attributes. In this example, the first -rw tells us that the owner has read and write (i.e., edit) permissions, the group also has read and write permissions, and all others can read, but not write the file.

```
$ ls -l
-rw-rw-r-- 1 ubuntu ubuntu 0 Jan 14 00:33 newfile
```

You can edit permissions using chmod. This example will add (+) write permissions to others (o).

```
$ chmod o+w
$ ls -l
-rw-rw-rw- 1 ubuntu ubuntu 0 Jan 14 00:33 newfile
```

You can also use chown to change an object's ownership. Right now, as you can see, the file is owned by the ubuntu user and belongs to the ubuntu group. This command will transfer ownership to a user account named steve, while leaving the object in the ubuntu group.

```
$ sudo chown steve:ubuntu newfile
$ ls -l
-rw-rw-rw- 1 steve ubuntu 0 Jan 14 00:33 newfile
```

8.5.4   Help

One last thing. When you run into trouble, your first stop will probably be the internet...and for good reason. But don't ignore the wealth of helpful information available to you on the Linux command line through the **man** system. Typing **man** followed by name of the command you're stuck on will open a well arranged guide to the command's use.

$ man chmod

Figure 8.3 shows the first screenful of goodness from the man file on **chmod**.

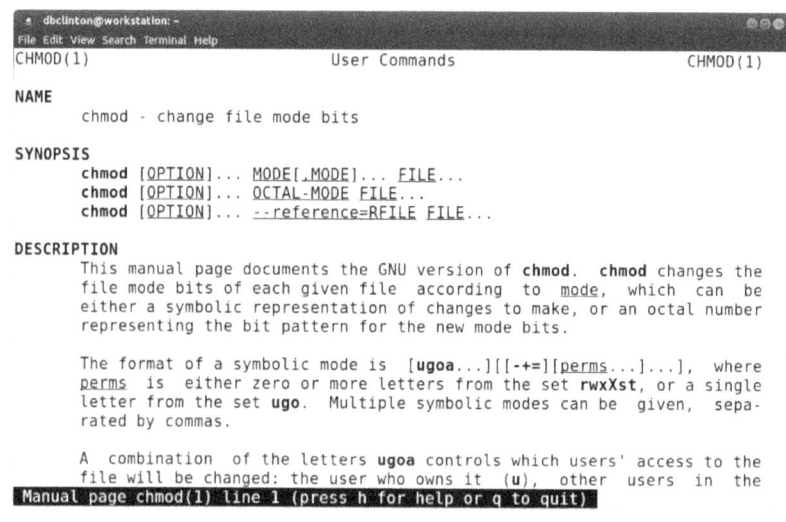

Figure 8.3: The first screen from the man file for chmod

Chapter 9

Appendix 3: Amazon Web Services

Does Amazon Web Services - Amazon's cloud computing platform - also deserve my "big tent" designation? Perhaps not. By any metric I can imagine, this is a tent that's far *too large* to pitch anywhere in the known galaxy. We're going to need a bigger metaphor.

What's this AWS all about? Here's how I describe it in my Learn Amazon Web Services in a Month of Lunches book:

> Suppose you didn't want to purchase, build, and house all the expensive hardware you'd need to properly support your new e-commerce website. Perhaps you're not sure how successful the project will be, so investing heavily in server, cooling, and routing equipment doesn't make sense. But if you could rent just enough of *someone else's* equipment to match the fast-changing ups and downs in demand on your site and pay only for what you actually used, then it might work.

> Is there anyone out there who might rent you this kind of stuff? Yup. They're called cloud computing providers. And Amazon's Amazon Web Services (AWS) is by far the most feature-rich and (generating nearly $12 billion in revenue in 2016) successful player in the market.

> According to the research firm Gartner (http://mng.bz/31dr),

AWS "has the largest share of compute capacity in use by paying customers - many times the aggregate size of all other providers in the market... It has the richest array of IaaS and PaaS capabilities. It provides the deepest capabilities for governing a large number of users and resources. It continues to rapidly expand its service offerings and to offer higher-level solutions."

AWS has proven itself capable of providing a secure and reliable hosting platform for both mission-critical (e-commerce, enterprise intranets) and compute-intensive (big data analytics, development environments) applications. Given its depth, if your project can be virtualized in one form or another then, according to Gartner, AWS is "the safe choice."

Ok. So how does it work? Well that depends on what you want to accomplish and how much time and energy you're willing to invest up front.

You see, it would be fairly simple to precisely replicate your on-premises infrastructure using AWS resources with a relatively soft learning curve. Basically, anything you can do on your own bare metal servers, you can do on AWS. Sometimes, it's even possible to create an archive of your application and databases and transfer them to the cloud with a single command.

But you won't always get the best bang for your buck that way. To really squeeze very ounce of value out of the AWS compute and database instances you provision, you'll usually need to reshape your application to take advantage of the cloud's built-in scalabilty and elasticity. Digging deeper, you might find that you don't even need compute or database instances, but can, instead, run your app in "thin air" - serverless.

This chapter won't even try to teach you *how* to do all that - read my Manning book Learn Amazon Web Services in a Month of Lunches book for all that stuff. Rather, I'll try to introduce you to the architectural principles that drive successful AWS workloads.

Read on.

9.1 Migrating workloads

An application server, when everything's said and done, is nothing but an application server. Slap some RAM, storage, a network interface, and an operating system on top of a healthy CPU and hit the power switch. Should you really care where it all happens to live?

An AWS account provides you with all the virtual compute instances you could want through their Elastic Compute Cloud (EC2) service. As figure 9.1 shows, you get to choose the pre-installed operating system you want to provision - or create your own custom machine images. You will also be able to set an instance type (the hardware profile you want to run), network environment, storage resources, and firewall settings (called a security group). Total time from start to launch: ~30 seconds when going with default values.

Figure 9.1: Select a pre-installed operating system image for a new AWS EC2 instance you can subsequently launch

Once your server is running, you can access it remotely - usually via SSH - and set about getting your application going. Keep an eye on things during the testing/transition period to see what might need changing.

- Is your instance too frail to handle the load? Upgrade it with a few clicks.

- Does your application rely on lots of large media files? Store them for less on Amazon's Simple Storage Service (S3).
- Is your server sitting idle for many hours each day? Shut it down and schedule a start up for when you'll need it...and save a boatload of money in the process.

Simple servers really aren't at all difficult to build. But optimizing more complex infrastructure is a bit of a science.

9.2 Refactoring and optimizing cloud workloads

Figuring out how to effectively tweak your cloud-based resources requires a solid understanding of two sometimes misunderstood concepts. This should help:

Elasticity is a system's ability to monitor user demand and automatically increase and decrease deployed resources accordingly. This quality is a big part of cloud computing's secret sauce, as it's what lets you design and deploy an application. You can be confident that the cloud provider will invisibly provision or retire resources according to need, ensuring that you never get stuck with the bill for unused services.

Scalability describes the way a system is designed to meet changing demand. That means the underlying design supports rapid, unpredictable changes. As an example, software that's scalable can be easily picked up and dropped onto a new server - possibly in a new network environment - and run without any manual configuration. Or, in other words, the composition of a scalable infrastructure can be quickly changed in a way that all the old bits and pieces immediately know how to work together with the new ones.

To function as true cloud-native applications, your code needs to understand the automated nature of its environment and be able to instantly adapt to changes.

On AWS, this might include deploying your servers behind an Elastic Load Balancer (ELB). The balancer directs incoming requests to instances running in as part of an Auto Scaling group. The group, in turn, automates the process of modifying the number of running instances up and down to meet demand. Figure 9.2 shows the Policy page, part of the Auto Scaling configuration process. Here you define events you want to trigger the launch of a new instances. In this case, when existing servers reach 80% CPU capacity, another one will be started.

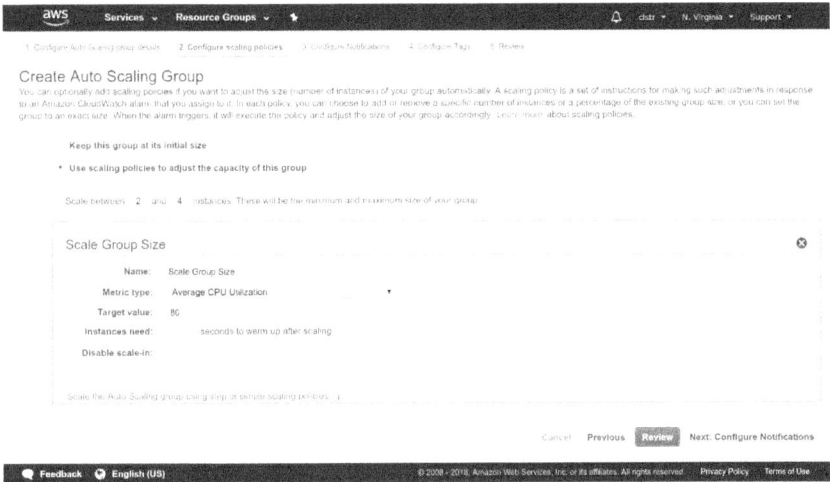

Figure 9.2: A scaling group will automatically launch or retire pre-configured instances according to changing demand

9.3 Serverless workloads

Serverless? What can you do without a server? Nothing, actually. But rather than renting an entire virtual server instance they way you would through EC2, in the "serverless" world you rent just a second or two of time on one of AWS's own servers. Since the mechanics of the whole thing are less visible, we call the process "serverless."

The primary AWS implementation of serverless computing is called Lambda. It currently lets you create functions in Node.js, C#, Java, and Python. Lambda is deeply integrated with a wide range of AWS services - both as triggers to invoke and Lambda function, and as resources to be used as part of a function.

The idea is that events happening in other AWS services can be configured

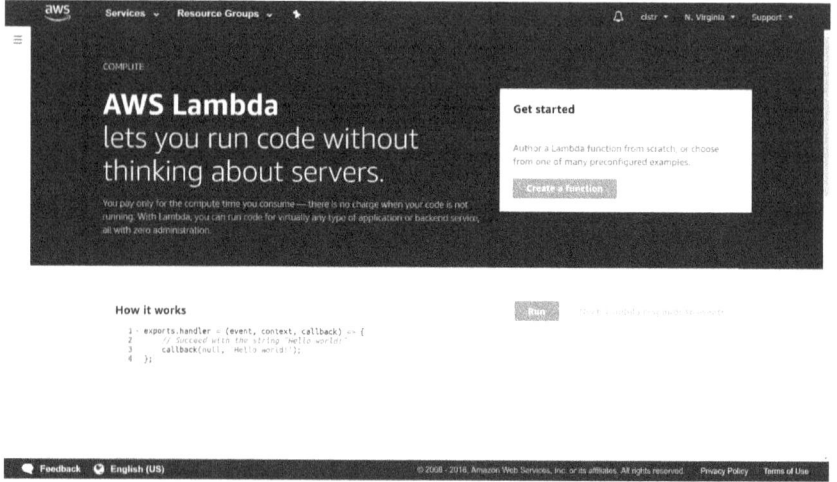

Figure 9.3: The AWS Lambda intro page. That Run button will actually fire up a live function

to trigger the quick execution of a function using only the bare minimum of cloud resources needed to spawn an action. The classic example to illustrate the way it works is the old generate-a-thumbnail-from-an-image-file trick; and really, who *doesn't* need to generate thumbnails from images every now and then?

Here's how it goes: whenever a customer of your online image storage business saves a photograph to your S3 bucket, a Lambda function springs to life, creates a small thumbnail version of the image, saves it to a second bucket, and associates the two images so the thumbnail will appear as a link to the original in website displays. You don't need to run (and pay for) an entire EC2 instance 24 hours a day just in case someone's wedding photos show up. Instead, you run exactly what you need, exactly when you need it.

Chapter 10

Wrapping it all up

So that's serverless computing, AWS, big tent technologies...and the whole range of tools and tricks for successfully achieving all of your learning goals. My bit's done now.

But I invite you to pick up where I've left off. Do you see something I've missed or a mistake, large or small? Please let me know. The internet is only as useful as all of us together decide to make it.

Know someone who might like this book? Please pass it along - either a digital or printed version. Want to share your thoughts about the book? Consider writing a review on Amazon.

And be in touch. Don't be a stranger.

David Clinton bootstrap-it.com office@bootstrap-it.com

www.ingramcontent.com/pod-product-compliance
Lightning Source LLC
Chambersburg PA
CBHW071237170526
45165CB00003B/1129